Psychiatric Drugs

Psychiatric Drugs is published in association with
Mind (National Association for Mental Health)
15–19 Broadway, London E15 4BQ

Mind has been speaking out for better mental health for 60 years. We work in partnership with around 200 local Mind associations to directly improve the lives of people with experience of mental distress. Mental health problems affect people from every ethnic background and walk of life – one in four people experience mental distress at some time in their lives and a third of all GP visits relate to mental health.

Mind believes everyone is entitled to the care they need in order to live a full life and to play their full part in society. Our vision is of a society that promotes and protects good mental health for all, and that treats people with experience of mental distress fairly, positively and with respect.

Our independence from pharmaceutical companies and government gives us the freedom to speak out on important or controversial issues, where others may not be able to. We campaign to influence policy and legislation in England and Wales, work closely with the media and are the first source of unbiased, independent mental health information via our publications, website www.mind.org.uk and phone service Mind*info*Line 0845 766 0163.

The points of view expressed in this publication do not necessarily reflect Mind policy.

Psychiatric Drugs

Key Issues and Service User Perspectives

Jim Read

**For better
mental health**

First published 2009 by
PALGRAVE MACMILLAN

Palgrave Macmillan in the UK is an imprint of Macmillan Publishers Limited,
registered in England, company number 785998, of Houndmills, Basingstoke,
Hampshire RG21 6XS.

Palgrave Macmillan in the US is a division of St Martin's Press LLC,
175 Fifth Avenue, New York, NY 10010.

Palgrave Macmillan is the global academic imprint of the above companies
and has companies and representatives throughout the world.

Palgrave® and Macmillan® are registered trademarks in the United States,
the United Kingdom, Europe and other countries.

ISBN 13: 978–0–230–54940–1 paperback
ISBN 10: 0–230–54940–3 paperback

This book is printed on paper suitable for recycling and made from fully
managed and sustained forest sources. Logging, pulping and manufacturing
processes are expected to conform to the environmental regulations of the
country of origin.

A catalogue record for this book is available from the British Library.

A catalog record for this book is available from the Library of Congress.

10 9 8 7 6 5 4 3 2 1
18 17 16 15 14 13 12 11 10 09

Printed and bound in China

Contents

Tables

Critical Reflection Boxes

Acknowledgements

Alison Cobb at Mind and Catherine Gray at Palgrave made this book possible. Special thanks go to Veronica Dewan for her multifarious contributions to the entire project.

Thanks to the people who contributed to the 'Coping with coming off' survey which forms some of the content of this book. Members of the research team in various capacities were Indra Dewan, Veronica Dewan, Alison Faulkner, Jolie Goodman, Raza Griffiths, Rosemary Harris, Eileen Philip, Mina Sassoon, Kate Summerside, Premila Trivedi and Jan Wallcraft. Members of the advisory group were Peter Campbell, Catherine Clarke, Katherine Darton, Diane Denton, Charanjit Dosanjh, Portia Omo-Bare, Kerry Sproston and Phil Thomas. Thanks to the people we interviewed for sharing their experiences, and especially to the three people who agreed to their stories being included here in some detail. The survey was made possible through a grant from the Department of Health. Angela Sweeney provided additional data analysis of the survey for this book.

The author would like to acknowledge the kind permission of the copyright holders for permission to use the following material: the Scottish Association for Mental Health (SAMH) for extensive use of data and quotes from their 2004 report '"All you need to know?": Scottish survey of people's experience of psychiatric drugs'; Datapharm Communications Ltd for data from the Medicines Guide on citalopram, 'hydrobromide when used for depression', www.medicines.org.uk, used in Table 1.1.

Thanks to Guy Holmes, Marese Hudson and Openmind for use of an extract from 'Coming off medication?' used in Critical Reflection Box 4.1. Staff at Mind helped with numerous enquiries; Katherine Darton commented on the first draft and Fiona Lynch assisted with research. Juanita Bullough and Kate Llewellyn of Palgrave contributed to the completion of this book. Thanks also to Carolyn Roberts of the Scottish Association for Mental Health for her assistance and the following people for responding to my email enquiries: Clive Ballard, Malcolm Black, Elizabeth Fox, Juliette Harrison, Robin Henne, Kathleen Heppell, Martin Jones, Shameem Mir, Isla Rippon, Trevor H. Turner, Bridget Winkle.

Introduction

This is a book about psychiatric drugs written from a fresh perspective; that of people who have taken them. My interest in the subject stems from my own experience of being on psychiatric drugs and many years of discussing them with friends and colleagues in the mental health system survivor or service users' movement. Much of the content of this book relies on people's willingness to talk openly about their experiences, and in my working life as a trainer, writer, researcher and consultant on issues of concern to service users, I developed the principle of not asking people to share information I wasn't prepared to share myself, so I will begin this introduction with a brief account of my own psychiatric drugs story.

After an early childhood encounter with barbiturates, from the ages of 19 to 21 I was on tranquillisers and antidepressants. It was a long time ago, in the 1970s, and a small story compared with those of people who have been on them (or on and off them) for decades, but for me it was a major event which had a profound effect on the rest of my life.

The prescribing and taking of psychiatric drugs is always about more than a chemical and a brain, and this is illustrated by the circumstances in which I started taking them. I had failed to study for university exams and was sent to a doctor who would assess whether I was simply lazy (bad) or ill (mad). The prescription of antidepressants was part of a diagnostic package that legitimised my failure to take the exams and gave me another opportunity. Soon I was on tranquillisers as well but I never did find the concentration and will to study. After a few months I had a brief adventure, working in a restaurant in Florida in the USA. Life was so busy and demanding that I kept forgetting to take my pills and stopped them altogether. But after a relationship went badly I went back on my pills and returned to England. My attempts to get my life on track seemed thwarted at every turn and I ended up as an informal day patient. I happened to live within walking distance of one of the old asylums – Park Prewitt in Basingstoke, southern England – and would go there to take part in occupational therapy.

The drugs I was taking hadn't made a big impact on me until I was taken off the tricyclic antidepressant and put on another type of antidepressant rarely used now called a monoamine-oxidase inhibitor (MAOI). These had a strong sedative effect on me. One day my parents went out to work, came back and I hadn't moved. They took me up to the hospital and the doctor decided I must be on too high a dose and reduced it. By this time I was sinking into the role of chronic mental patient, but all this changed when I was told that as the drugs hadn't worked I was to have ECT (electroconvulsive therapy).

Up until this time I had done what I was told but, having seen the effects of ECT on fellow patients, I somehow found the ability to refuse and stopped going to the hospital. My family doctor suggested that instead I should move to a therapeutic community called Cassel Hospital, where I would live with other young people and get help with my problems. I agreed, was assessed and accepted, and told I had to come off my drugs before I moved in. I was given no warnings or advice about coming off the drugs, stopped them overnight and felt nothing worse that a bit shaky. It wasn't until the 1980s that I became aware that tranquillisers could be highly addictive and only when researching for this book did I discover that coming off MAOI antidepressants abruptly can cause life-threatening reactions (Glenmullen 2005, pp. 211–12). Had I encountered difficulties in stopping these drugs (and lived!) I might well have gone back on them and my life could have taken a very different course.

Instead I spent eight months living in the therapeutic community before attempting, with eventual success, to live independently and build a new life for myself. I hadn't completely bought in to the idea of not using psychiatric drugs though. I have memories from the period after I left the Cassel of lying in bed phoning A&E (accident and emergency) departments asking for tranquillisers only to be defeated by their refusal to dispatch supplies by courier. As things turned out, though, the only psychiatric drugs I have ingested since then have been the occasional tranquilliser, prescribed for emergency pain relief.

Even within this short story are themes that regularly crop up in people's accounts of taking psychiatric drugs: passivity, indifference, stopping and starting, over-prescribing, adverse effects, ignorance about coming off them and insecurity about managing without them. But whereas my experience of drugs was basically negative, others have more positive stories to tell. Twenty five years of being involved in the movement of service users or survivors of psychiatry has taught me that for every person who says their life has been ruined by psychiatric drugs there is someone who believes they have been saved by them, and many more who just don't know, who have been taking them for years and wonder if their lives would have been better or worse if they had been free of them.

Listening to Service Users

When I was a mental patient no-one was interested in what I had to say about the treatment I received. This was partly to do with the paternalism of the medical profession – 'doctor knows best' – and applied equally to other branches of medicine. Mental hospitals were strict hierarchies, with psychiatrists on top and everyone telling the people below them what to do until you got to the patient at the bottom. Mental patients were, anyway, considered too irrational to have valid views about their treatment or the circumstances of their lives.

But in the UK, the 1980s were a time of upheaval in mental health services, as the old asylums were replaced by community facilities such as day centres and supported housing projects. People who had been hidden away in institutions found themselves living in ordinary communities with a degree of independence. These changes may have contributed to a situation in which users of mental health services felt more able to advocate on their own behalf. Self-organisation wasn't new, but began to flourish more than ever before. The UK-wide organisation, Survivors Speak Out, was formed and was soon campaigning against proposals to extend compulsory treatment to include some people living in the community. Local organisations set up patients' councils and advocacy projects (Survivor/User History Group 2008).

This self-organisation reflected and benefited from similar activities that were already under way elsewhere. In the USA the closing of asylums had begun earlier and in her book, *On Our Own* (1988), first published in 1977, Judi Chamberlain described community projects there and in Canada that were controlled by service users. In the Netherlands, patients' councils were well established and people who were organising them helped to get them started in the UK (Read & Wallcraft 1994).

Another strand of action was more focused on primary care. People who had been taking tranquillisers, such as diazepam (Valium), for years were realising they had become addicted to them despite denials from drug companies and doctors. They formed self-help groups to support each other to get off the drugs and spoke out in the media (Lacey and Woodward 1985; Medawar 1992).

The UK NHS and Community Care Act 1990 required service providers to consult with users of their services and their 'carers' (meaning family members). With associated funding for local groups becoming more available this gave a new impetus to the activities of service users. But with it came a different emphasis. Instead of deciding on their own priorities and campaigns, service users were being asked to respond to more limited agendas set by bureaucratic organisations.

'User involvement', as it came to be known, has been far from an unqualified success (Read 2001; Wallcraft, Read & Sweeney 2003; Campbell 2005) but has established the legitimacy of service users' views. A succession of policy directives has introduced user involvement into every aspect of the planning and provision of mental health services (Department of Health 1999), the education and training professionals (Postgraduate Medical Education and Training Board 2008) and people's own treatment plans through the Care Programme Approach, introduced in 1991 (Department of Health 2008).

Through their own initiative and the encouragement of others service users have also involved themselves in just about every other aspect of mental health services, from running self-help groups to setting up crisis houses, and from evaluating services to organising activities to promote their own emotional well-being (Wallcraft, Read & Sweeney 2003).

The publication of this book is a product of these last 20 years and more of intense and continuous activity by service users, and by professionals, policy makers and politicians promoting user involvement. Funding from the Department of Health for the original research – Coping with Coming Off – included here, and the decision by a leading mental health organisation, Mind, to commission the research from a group of current and former service users reflect and help to create a climate in which the contribution of 'experts by experience' is becoming more welcomed and expected.

For an academic publisher to produce a book written by someone whose expertise stems from his personal experience of the mental health system and immersion in the service users' movement rather than formal training and academic qualifications is a bold step, but one that can be justified in an era in which mental health professionals are expected to familiarise themselves with the views of service users.

Service Users and Research

Another aspect of the mental health world to which service users are making an increasing contribution is research. We have moved from being merely the subjects of research to participants who are asked to describe our experiences and say what we think, and on to initiating and carrying out research projects.

Two psychiatrists, Patrick Bracken and Philip Thomas, identify why it matters that we have done this. In their book, *Postpsychiatry: Mental Health in a Postmodern World* (2005, p. 51), they point out that user-led research in mental health is unique. There is no equivalent in general medicine. They suggest that it has developed 'out of frustration with the failure of professional-led research to engage with issues and outcomes that are important to service users'.

User-led research has been an especially strong feature of service-user activity in the UK, exemplified by two projects, Strategies for Living, based at the Mental Health Foundation and SURE (Service User Research Enterprise) with the Institute of Psychiatry.

Nearly all research into psychiatric drugs is initiated and funded by drug companies and their priority is to prove that their products are safe and effective in order to be able to bring them on to the market and sell them in profitable amounts. To prove effectiveness they have to be able to demonstrate that the drugs reduce symptoms associated with the various diagnoses of mental illness without also producing unacceptable adverse effects. In practice these drugs trials only measure their short term effects.

People who take psychiatric drugs want to know these things, but may be equally concerned with others. For example, they may want to know what harm taking them may do over time, how long they have to take them for and whether they will have trouble stopping them – information that is under-researched and may be slow to emerge. Above all they want to know if the overall effect of taking psychiatric drugs is likely to have a positive or negative impact on their lives. Professionals who prescribe them, make sure people are taking them and support people who are on them should, of course, be equally interested in their overall impact.

Finding answers to these questions is not straightforward. Over time there are many factors that influence people's mental and physical health. How to identify the effects of one intervention? There is no perfect method, but people with the lived experience of that intervention can make a strong contribution. When the intervention is a psychiatric drug and the people taking it are diagnosed as mentally ill, the issue of credibility arises. But although our views were once deemed to be inevitably irrational because of our 'madness' or 'neurosis', we have now established credibility as commentators on our own lives. The annual survey of service users' views carried out by the Healthcare Commission

(Healthcare Commission 2008a) as a measure of the performance of providers of mental health services is testament to our newfound status.

But issues of credibility remain. The only way to systematically gather, analyse and present people's accounts of their experience is through well-designed surveys. But surveys do not have a high status in the traditional world of academic research. For example, in the original hierarchy of 'clinical evidence' considered by NICE (the National Institute for Health and Clinical Excellence) when evaluating treatments, they did not feature at all (Eccles & Mason, cited in Snowden 2008, p. 92). If our views have credibility but the only method of ascertaining them does not, then we are still sidelined and a contribution to the understanding of psychiatric drugs is lost.

All research methods have their limitations, including the so-called 'gold standard' of research: the double-blind, randomised controlled trial. Assessors of evidence could do with taking on board the extensive criticisms of this method (discussed in Chapter 1) and being more open to findings from surveys. Similarly, when considering complex interactions, there is a role for the qualitative data that emerge from in-depth interviews as well as quantitative data – numbers and percentages.

Few mental health workers will have ever seen a survey of people's views on their experiences of psychiatric drugs. Yet without this information there are gaping holes in our picture of how much they affect people's mental and emotional well-being. As David Healy (2005, p. xii), a renowned expert on psychiatric drugs and critic of drug companies, has said, 'The final arbiter of whether psychotropic medication is useful or not is the taker.'

The Coping with Coming Off Research

The core of this book comprises three chapters on a research project looking at people's experiences of trying to come off their medication. This may appear to be rather specific for a book intended for people who want to educate themselves more generally about psychiatric drugs. But there are two reasons for including it. First, although the focus is coming off drugs, this includes much valuable description of interactions between the mental health workers who prescribe the drugs and try to ensure they are taken and the people they prescribe them to. Secondly, the issues of withdrawal from psychiatric drugs are vitally important to service users. Nearly everyone who takes a psychiatric drug will stop taking it at some point. Will they get ill again? Will they find they have become addicted to it? Will the doctor agree to them stopping and, if not, should they do it anyway? These crucial questions are given relatively little attention in the literature about psychiatric drugs.

Coping with Coming Off (CWCO) is an in-depth survey of just over 200 people. The most comprehensive survey of users' views and experiences is by the Scottish Association for Mental Health and published as *"All you need to know?"* (SAMH 2004). Over 1000 people filled in questionnaires about every aspect of their recent experience of psychiatric drugs. With these numbers it is possible to compare people's experiences of different drugs within the same type. Material from this survey has been used to augment that from CWCO.

Relevance to Current Trends

Mental health services are changing. In England, since the publication of the *National Service Framework for Mental Health* in 1999 (Department of Health 1999) there have been a host of initiatives aimed at providing more effective community-based services. At the same time changes affecting all health services are taking place, with the emphasis on providing patients with more choice. Policy doesn't always translate into practice, as exemplified by difficulties in involving people in decisions about their own care and treatment through the care-programme approach. In 2008 a survey found that only 40 per cent of people with a care plan said they had definitely been involved in deciding it, with 36 per cent saying they had been involved to some extent and 24 per cent saying they had not been involved at all (Healthcare Commission 2008a, tables section F).

But although the rhetoric may be ahead of the reality, there are so many policy documents, projects and campaigns that it is beginning to seem inevitable that there will be significant changes in relationships between doctors and patients, with the prescribing of psychiatric drugs (or decisions not to prescribe) becoming more often more of a joint decision between doctor and patient.

Three initiatives in particular are indicative of these changing roles. These are:

- guidelines on shared decision-making and adherence in prescribing;
- new roles for mental health workers; and
- widespread adoption of the recovery approach in mental health services.

Doctors prescribing medicines which their patients don't take has been a common phenomenon, not restricted to the mental health world. Traditionally this behaviour by patients has been known as non-compliance and been viewed by health workers as mistaken and in need of correction. But a new approach has been developed which acknowledges patients' rights to discuss and negotiate with prescribers and ultimately to make their own decisions.

A NICE clinical guideline, *Medicines Adherence: Involving patients in decisions about prescribed medicines and supporting adherence* (2009a), describes a new and more equal relationship between prescribers and patients which emphasises the importance of prescribers listening to patients' concerns about medication and seeking to reach agreement with them. (There is more about shared decision-making and adherence in Chapter 1.)

In England, the roles of mental health workers are changing. One clear, obvious and definite change is the extension of 'non-medical' prescribing. From 2006 suitably qualified nurses and pharmacists have been able to independently prescribe nearly all licensed medicines (Department of Health, 2006a, p. 4). Similar arrangements have since been introduced in the rest of the UK.

In other ways, also, professional hierarchies and barriers are breaking down. A Department of Health initiative, 'New Ways of Working' (Department of Health 2007, p. 11), is intended to enhance team working and, for example, encourages staff 'to share knowledge, skills and competences across professional and practitioner boundaries'. Dr Joanna Bennett, Senior Research Fellow at the Sainsbury Centre for Mental Health, suggests (2008, p. 122) that mental health practitioners – and not just those with prescribing powers – need 'knowledge of the effectiveness of medication and at least a working knowledge of psychopharmacology' to enable 'discussion amongst the multidisciplinary team members and the service user on the most effective use of medication and the integration of different treatment approaches'. Gone are the days when mental health workers simply left the business of medication to doctors.

The Department of Health has produced a leaflet to explain 'New Ways of Working' to patients and carers (Department of Health 2007). Among the reasons listed for bringing in this initiative are: 'it moves away from attitudes of dominance and control' and 'service users can be seen as a whole person and not just an illness'.

The third of these current trends is the widespread adoption of the recovery approach. It can be an elusive concept and is not necessarily about 'cure' but more about leading the fullest life you possibly can. The recovery approach emphasises the significance of hope for people diagnosed with long-term conditions. In mental health, avoiding passivity and taking charge of your own destiny are important components that challenge aspects of traditional services.

Pat Deegan, a service user from the USA, should be credited with having done much to develop the recovery approach. New Zealand and the state of Wisconsin in the USA have pioneered the adoption of this approach by services (New Zealand Mental Health Commission 2001; Jacobson, cited in SCIE 2007, p. 14). Now it is achieving widespread acceptance in the UK. For example, a review of mental health nursing, *From values to action* (Department of Health 2006b, p. 4), states that 'Mental health nursing should incorporate the broad principles of the Recovery Approach into every aspect of their practice'. The Royal College of Psychiatrists is also supporting adoption of the recovery approach and is committed to training psychiatrists to work in this way (2008, p. 27).

The recovery approach does not include a specific view on psychiatric drugs but does emphasise choice, with professionals being more willing to take the lead from patients. The Royal College of Psychiatrists (2008, p. 29) goes as far as to say that mental health workers 'should support people in trying to achieve the goals they set for themselves, even if they believe the goals are not realistic'. Presumably this includes goals about living without medication.

These three trends are consistent with each other, with service-user action and involvement, and the Care Programme Approach. All have implications for how decisions about psychiatric drugs are made. People who have been non-compliant with medication regimes have to be respected, negotiated with and their right to refuse acknowledged.

Except, of course, mental health legislation allows the service user to be overruled in certain circumstances. A challenge for services working in new ways is to not allow this power to contaminate situations in which it doesn't apply.

Purpose and Scope of the Book

I have written this book primarily for people studying to work in mental health services. I hope it will help them to engage in the confusing and contentious world of use of psychiatric drugs from a perspective that starts with the experiences and concerns of service users.

Everyone involved in providing mental health services in the statutory and voluntary (non-governmental) services needs to understand the place of psychiatric drugs in the lives of the people with whom they work. This includes staff who have most day-to-day contact with service users and who potentially have the best understanding of how they are experiencing medication and how they feel about it.

Throughout the book are boxes containing ideas for critical reflection. These can be used by students on their own or in groups. Ideally a student should make notes and use them to contribute to a discussion.

No prior knowledge of psychiatric drugs is required to understand this book. There is a brief guide to the different types in Chapter 1. When I have needed to use medical terms I have explained them.

I hope that this book will also find a wider audience. It is not a conventional basic guide and offers something new to anyone involved in the mental health field. The CWCO research offers new angles on old problems that are relevant to current issues such as choice, recovery and listening to service users. There are implications for policy at local and national (or state) level.

It is not written as a self-help book but does include material that will be of interest to anyone who is thinking about coming off their psychiatric drugs and which will help them to make informed decisions about whether and how to proceed. This material will also benefit anyone who takes on the responsibility of advising and supporting someone who is thinking of stopping their drugs. I suggest also that people who have family members and friends on psychiatric drugs could benefit from reading it.

I have been unable to locate any significant surveys of people's experiences and views of psychiatric drugs from outside the UK. But I think the UK research has relevance for any country where psychiatric drugs are used. I have taken other research and sources of information from wherever I can find them. They include much from the USA. Most of the organisations, regulations and guidelines mentioned are from the UK and I have not assumed that all readers are familiar with them.

I do not attempt to explain the biochemical action of drugs on the brain and rest of the body. Instead I focus on why and how they are used, the people who take them and how they deal with the people who prescribe them and monitor their use.

Also beyond the scope of this book is the use of drugs with young people under 18, for whom different guidelines apply.

Structure of the Book

Chapter 1 sets the scene. It begins with an overview of the place of drug treatments in mental health services and introduces the drugs most commonly used in psychiatry. It then looks at how they are supposed to be used according to current guidance, how current practice diverges from these guidelines and at criticisms of the guidelines.

Then I identify the following five key issues concerning the use of psychiatric drugs:

1. Adverse effects of psychiatric drugs: What are their range, severity and frequency, and what impact do they have on the lives of people taking them?
2. Choice and compulsion: What rights do people have to be informed about and exercise choice over drugs they are prescribed, what powers do psychiatrists have to force people to take drugs, and how are the tensions between choice and compulsion played out in practice?
3. People from black and minority ethnic (BME) communities: What are the issues about over-prescribing of psychiatric drugs for people in BME communities, what is being done about them, and what more could be done?
4. The rise and possible fall of SSRI antidepressants: Some of the problems with drugs being manufactured and marketed for profit are epitomised by the way the popularity of Prozac and similar antidepressants has outweighed their actual effectiveness and safety. How did this occur, and what is the future for these drugs?
5. Effectiveness: What are the challenges in measuring the effectiveness of psychiatric drugs, and is there an evidence base to justify their dominant position in the treatment of mental distress?

Chapter 2 re-examines these key issues from the perspectives of people who have taken the drugs. By drawing on key surveys from the UK it brings in a perspective that is usually lacking in discussion and decision making about psychiatric drugs. From this we learn about the impact of adverse effects on people's lives and what they are prepared to tolerate if they feel they are benefiting from the drugs. We see people's assessments of how good mental health workers are at giving information about what they can expect from taking psychiatric drugs, with examples of good and bad practice. Service users from BME communities talk about how they feel cajoled into taking drugs they don't like and how they perceive this as racism. People who have taken fluoxetine and similar drugs give their verdicts, and we see how they are compared with other approaches, such as talking treatments. Finally, we see how people rate all the different types of psychiatric drugs for overall helpfulness and how people taking the same drugs can experience them very differently.

In Chapter 3 we look at the three stages of coming off, or attempting to come off, psychiatric drugs. These start with the decision to come off. What does clinical guidance say about how long people should stay on their medication, and what happens in practice? The second stage is what people experience during the process of coming off. Included here is a discussion of the concepts and language of addiction and dependence, and a look at how to distinguish between symptoms returning as the effects of drugs wear off and withdrawal syndromes. The third stage is about what happens to people who succeed in coming off psychiatric drugs. Do they tend to flourish, relapse, or carry on much as before?

This is followed by three chapters based on the Coping with Coming Off (CWCO) research. In Chapter 4 I describe how the research was carried out and who the people were who participated. Then there is a detailed look at people's reasons for trying to come off their drugs. We also see how they went about making the decision and, in particular, how they did or did not involve their doctors and their reasons why. Chapter 5 includes material on the experience of trying to come off – how hard it was and what support people received. We also look at what factors influenced success; factors such as whether or not they told their doctor, what drugs they were on, and how long they had been taking them for. Then we see what benefits were felt by people who succeeded and what lessons were learned by people who didn't succeed.

One of the most significant themes that emerges from the research is the tension between doctors and patients diagnosed with schizophrenia or bipolar disorder about whether they should stay on their medication. In Chapter 6, this is explored in depth, with the stories of three participants in the research used to illustrate how these tensions are played out and can sometimes be resolved.

In Chapter 7 I return to the five key issues, look further at how they are informed by the experiences and views of people taking psychiatric drugs, and make some suggestions for improving practice. The conclusion draws together hopeful thoughts about a new relationship between people who prescribe, administer and monitor medication and the people who they may prescribe it for.

Appendix 1 lists resources for people wanting practical guidance about coming off psychiatric drugs and Appendix 2 brings together some statistics to show what proportions of people experience unwanted effects when stopping different drugs.

Language

Anyone writing about mental health issues indicates their own orientation and beliefs by the language they use. The choices I make here reflect my involvement in the service users (or should that be survivors?) movement. Above all, we want to be seen as people and not be defined by diagnosis. We are not schizophrenics but people diagnosed with schizophrenia, which includes people who do or don't accept the validity of the diagnosis. I sometimes resort to 'service user' and 'patient' for conciseness and to avoid repetition, but have generally preferred 'people who have taken psychiatric drugs' and similar terms.

I refer to mental distress rather than mental illness because it is a more inclusive term as it doesn't assume a medical explanation. But I have used some contestable words and phrases from psychiatry without comment or inverted commas simply for convenience and clarity of text. They include psychosis and non-compliant. Other choices of language – such as neuroleptic or antipsychotic and withdrawal syndrome or discontinuation syndrome – I explain when they first occur.

I have used the general (generic) names for drugs, but if a drug is better known by its brand name I have included it in brackets the first time the drug is mentioned in each chapter, for example, 'fluoxetine (Prozac)'.

I use the terms 'over-prescribing' and 'over-medicating' several times and intend them to mean any of the following: prescribing drugs in higher doses or for longer than recommended in guidelines without justification; prescribing drugs in combinations that are not recommended in guidelines without justification; prescribing drugs at doses that don't take into account the possibility of the person metabolising them more slowly than average; continuing to prescribe drugs at doses or of types that are causing distress to the patient; wrongly prescribing neuroleptics or antimanics because the person has been misdiagnosed; prescribing drugs when other suitable courses of action exist which are preferred by the patient.

When I have reproduced material from elsewhere I have kept the original language.

A variety of terms and conventions are used when referring to people's skin colour or ethnic group. When referring to a particular report or article I have kept the terms and conventions used in it even when not quoting directly. I think and hope the inconsistency of language that results is less confusing than altering language from other sources.

Critical Reflection Box 1.1

Beliefs about Psychiatric Drugs

Take some time to examine your personal beliefs about psychiatric drugs by trying to answer the following questions. Don't be put off if you feel you don't know enough:

1. Think of the person you know best who has taken psychiatric drugs. What impact do you think they have made on that person's life? Do you and that person have the same opinion about them?
2. Can you think of someone for whom psychiatric drugs appear to have done more good than harm? If so, on what are you basing that judgement?
3. Can you think of an example of someone for whom psychiatric drugs appear to have done more harm than good? If so, on what are you basing that judgement?
4. Can you think of someone who isn't on psychiatric drugs who you think would benefit from taking them? What would you like to say to them?
5. Can you think of someone who is on psychiatric drugs who you think would benefit from coming off them? What would you like to say to them?
6. What has influenced your views about psychiatric drugs? Some possibilities are:

   (a) taking them yourself
   (b) seeing their effects on other people
   (c) professional training
   (d) your personal beliefs about dealing with life's challenges
   (e) other

7. And finally, how do you rate psychiatric drugs overall for helpfulness?

1

Overview and Key Issues

Overview

Drugs are the predominant form of treatment in mental health in the UK and other Western industrialised countries. It is unusual for somebody to be diagnosed as mentally ill and not be prescribed psychiatric drugs. A survey by the Healthcare Commission (2008a, tables section C) found that 93 per cent of people in England using community mental health services had been on medication in the previous 12 months.

The names of groups of psychiatric drugs suggest they have specific actions: antidepressants for depression, antimanics to stop people getting high, and so on. In fact, they have wide ranges of action and are used in a variety of ways. For example, some antimanic drugs are also anticonvulsants used to control epilepsy and some antidepressants are prescribed to control chronic pain. In her book, *The Myth of the Chemical Cure* (2007), Joanna Moncrieff argues that any benefits of psychiatric drugs derive from the sedation they cause rather than more specific action (although sedation may also be experienced as an adverse effect). In support of her thesis (pp. 78–9) she cites studies that suggest psychiatric drugs can be used interchangeably. For example tranquillisers, the antimanic drug, lithium, and even opium have been found to be similarly effective as 'antipsychotics' in reducing symptoms associated with the diagnosis of schizophrenia.

Even Samuel H. Barondes, Director of the Center for Neurobiology and Psychiatry at the University of California, who describes himself as an enthusiastic fan of psychiatric drugs, concedes (2005, p. xiv) that 'Even the best of them are blunt instruments that have a large number of effects on the brain, only some of which are therapeutic.'

When psychiatric drugs work well they reduce, or even eliminate, unwanted symptoms of distress. When someone enjoys their first proper sleep for weeks, their disturbing thoughts fade away or their chaotic behaviour is calmed; the drugs are doing their job. But such success is not guaranteed. People respond to drugs very differently. They may see no benefit at all, feel worse, or experience some improvement, but not as much as they hoped for.

The potential benefits have to be weighed against the possible adverse effects (or side effects). These vary from the unpleasant to the unbearable to the seriously harmful. Adjusting the dose or switching to another drug can improve the balance between desirable and undesirable effects.

People use all sorts of non-psychiatric drugs to affect their thoughts, mood and behaviour. They can broadly be classified into social drugs, which are generally acceptable and widely available, and street drugs, which are illegal and generally considered to be more dangerous. People may also turn to over-the-counter medicines and herbal remedies. Legally, there are strict demarcation lines between these types of drugs but, in practice, drugs don't always fit neatly into these categories. For example, tranquillisers are prescription drugs but may be obtained illegally and used with other street drugs (DrugScope 2008). The herbal antidepressant, St John's wort, is an over-the-counter medicine in the UK but widely prescribed by doctors in Germany. In Ireland it is only available on prescription (Brennan 2000).

All mood-altering drugs have in common the propensity to make people feel better or worse and to have adverse effects. They can be dangerous; people respond to them differently; it can be difficult to stop taking them.

Psychiatric drugs are not the only way of helping people who have been diagnosed as mentally ill. There is a wide range of therapies and activities with potential to make a difference. But the advantage psychiatric drugs have over all of them is convenience. They are easy to manufacture and distribute; a doctor can write a prescription and ten minutes later the patient has started a course of treatment. With some drugs, benefits may be apparent soon after beginning to take them. In comparison, talking treatments, for example, require the patient to turn up regularly for meetings with a trained therapist who has to be available at a suitable location and time. It may be weeks before any benefits are felt.

There is another clear distinction between psychiatric drugs and all other therapies and activities; the potential for profit. There is some profit to be made from the private provision of mental health services, but the big money is in drugs. The pharmaceutical industry is the UK's third most profitable economic activity after tourism and finance (House of Commons Health Committee 2005, p. 3). Pharmaceutical companies have a huge incentive to promote their products to doctors and the public. In the USA and New Zealand direct advertising of prescription drugs to the public is allowed (Redwood 2001). The companies have a particular incentive to promote their newer, and less proven, products when their right to exclusively manufacture them is protected by patent. In the market-place of ideas about what helps with mental health, the drug companies have considerable financial muscle to influence the debate.

Since 2003 the UK government agency responsible for overseeing and regulating the use of medical products, including psychiatric drugs, has been the Medicines and Healthcare products Regulatory Agency (MHRA).

NICE, the National Institute for Health and Clinical Excellence, assesses treatment options and produces technology appraisals and clinical guidelines. The appraisals are of specific treatments and the guidelines are about all approaches to treating particular illnesses and health problems. For example, NICE issued a technology appraisal of 'atypical antipsychotics' and a clinical guideline on core treatments for schizophrenia (NICE 2002a, 2002b).

The technology appraisals and clinical guidelines apply to England and Wales, and Northern Ireland subject to local review. Only multiple-technology appraisals (of more than one drug) apply to Scotland. (In Scotland, the Scottish Medicines Consortium produces guidance similar to single-technology appraisals and the Scottish Intercollegiate Guidelines Network produces clinical guidelines.)

Versions of the appraisals and guidelines are produced for patients and the public who also have access to the full versions through the website www.nice.org.uk. (As the focus of this book is the experience of people receiving treatments, quotes from NICE publications are from the versions for patients and the public, unless stated otherwise.) NICE guidance is highly relevant to issues highlighted in this book and so it is important to understand its status. This is what NICE has to say on the subject (2005a, p. 9):

> Once NICE publishes clinical guidance, health professionals and the organisations that employ them are expected to take it fully into account when deciding what treatments to give people. However, NICE guidance does not replace the knowledge and skills of individual health professionals who treat patients; it is still up to them to make decisions about a particular patient in consultation with the patient and/or their guardian or carer when appropriate.

Since January 2002, NHS organisations in England and Wales have been required to provide funding for medicines and treatments recommended by NICE in its technology appraisals guidance. (Since 2006 this has also applied to Northern Ireland.) The NHS normally has 3 months from the date of publication of each technology appraisal guidance to provide funding and resources. Local NHS organisations are expected to meet the costs of medicines and treatments recommended by NICE out of their general annual budgets.

When NICE publishes clinical guidelines, local health organisations should review their management of clinical conditions against the NICE guidelines. This review should consider the resources required to implement the guidelines, the people and processes involved, and how long it will take to do all this. It is in the interests of patients that the NICE recommendations are acted on as quickly as possible.

This means that technology appraisals have to be acted upon. This is intended to end 'postcode lotteries' whereby some treatments are only available in areas where health-service providers are prepared to pay for them. If, having tested a treatment for cost effectiveness, NICE says it should be used, then the money has to be found.

NHS trusts in England are monitored by the Care Quality Commission which, until 2009, was called the Healthcare Commission. It carries out regular checks on each trust and awards it an annual rating. Implementation of NICE technology appraisals is included in the core standards the trusts have to meet. Implementation of clinical guidelines is included in developmental standards, meaning that they have to show they are moving towards implementation.

The only statistics for drug use in England collected systematically are for the number of prescriptions dispensed in the community. Prescriptions from hospital pharmacies are not collected nationally and there are no statistics showing how many people are taking drugs and for how long. These prescription statistics do, however, demonstrate trends from year to year and comparisons of use between different drugs. Statistics for the other nations that make up the UK are collected separately. The situation is similar for the USA. The only national statistics available are estimates of the numbers of prescriptions dispensed in the community, and they are several years behind the figures for England.

DRUG GROUPS

Psychiatric drugs can be classified into four groups: tranquillisers, antidepressants, neuroleptics and antimanics. Within each group there are drug types. For example, antidepressants include tricyclics and selective serotonin reuptake inhibitors (SSRIs).

Tranquillisers

Tranquillisers are also known as 'minor tranquillisers' to distinguish them from major tranquillisers, a former name for neuroleptics. All but the most recent tranquillisers are in the chemical group benzodiazepines. When used to treat general anxiety, their medical name is anxiolytics, and when used as sleeping pills, their medical name is hypnotics. Those used as hypnotics tend to be shorter-acting than those used as anxiolytics. The intention is that someone taking them at night is not left feeling drugged the next morning. The newer tranquillisers, which are used as sleeping pills, are often called the Z-drugs, as their names are zaleplon, zolpidem and zopiclone.

Benzodiazepines were introduced at the beginning of the 1960s. They soon gained a reputation for being better than barbiturates, which were dangerous in overdose and addictive. But, before long, it became clear that tranquillisers could also be very difficult for people to stop taking, although the companies that made them tried to discredit the evidence. Further evidence emerged that they ceased to be effective after a few months (Medawar 1992). But sales soared, peaking at around 30 million prescriptions in Britain in 1977 (Medawar 1992, p. 101). It took until 1988 for the Committee on Safety of Medicines (a predecessor to the MHRA) to warn doctors to be more careful in prescribing these drugs. They were told tranquillisers should not be prescribed for more than four weeks at a time.

Since then, the number of prescriptions has fallen, but there is still evidence of widespread over-prescribing. From a poll carried out for the BBC TV programme *Panorama* (2001), it was estimated that over 1.5 million people in the UK had been taking tranquillisers for more than four months – way over the guideline of a maximum of four weeks, and by which time they are thought to be ineffective anyway. (This figure is presumably for the UK, although this information is not given in the transcript.) Nearly three-quarters (72 per cent) of these people had been prescribed their drugs in the previous ten years – since the guidance was issued. Between 2001 and 2007 annual prescriptions of tranquillisers fell by 600,000, but were still over 16 million (Department of Health 2002, pp. 99–102; Information Centre 2008, pp. 100–2).

In 2004, NICE issued clinical guidance on the management of panic disorder and generalised anxiety disorder in adults (NICE 2007a), which was amended in 2007. For both these conditions it said that psychological therapy, medicines and self-help have all been shown to be effective but that the benefits of psychological treatment last the longest. The psychological therapy that should be offered is Cognitive Behavioural Therapy (CBT). Benzodiazepines have no role in the management of panic disorder and should be used for a maximum of two to four weeks for the treatment of generalised anxiety disorder.

Also in 2004, NICE issued a technology appraisal on the use of Z-drugs for insomnia (NICE 2004a). It recommended that non-medical treatments should be considered first. It found there was no firm evidence that Z-drugs were more effective than benzodiazepines and so recommended that doctors prescribe the cheapest drug. In practice this is a benzodiazepine.

Tranquillisers can cause particularly severe problems for older people, even when prescribed according to the guidelines. Older people tend to metabolise drugs more slowly than younger people, causing them to accumulate in the body with a build-up of adverse effects. With tranquillisers this includes dizziness, which can cause falls. One study of sleeping pills (Busto, cited in BBC News 2005) suggested that the benefits to older people are so small compared with the adverse effects that there might not be any justification for prescribing them.

In 2007 there were 5.1 million prescriptions of Z-drugs in England, an increase of 500,000 since the technology appraisal was issued (Information Centre 2008, p. 101; 2005, p. 101). There were 4.9 million prescriptions of other hypnotics and 6.2 million prescriptions of anxiolytics (Information Centre 2008, pp. 100–2). In the USA, the number of prescriptions for tranquillisers was 39 million in 2004 (Stagnitti 2007, p. 2).

Antidepressants

Like tranquillisers, antidepressants were first introduced in the early 1960s. It is interesting to reflect that, before then, people somehow got by without these two widely prescribed groups of drugs. The first type of antidepressant was the tricyclic, which is still in use. The most significant development since then was the introduction of SSRIs in the late 1980s. These soon took over from tricyclics as the most frequently prescribed antidepressants. There are other types of antidepressant which are used quite rarely, the exception being venlafaxine (Efexor), which is a serotonin noradrenaline re-uptake inhibitor often tried when other antidepressants haven't worked. (See, for example, NICE 2007b, p. 37.)

NICE clinical guidelines demonstrate that SSRIs have become the first-choice antidepressant in most instances. They are used to treat not just depression, but other conditions that have been treated with benzodiazepines in the past. For example, if drug treatment is used for panic disorder it should be an SSRI, and they are also an option for generalised anxiety disorder (NICE 2007a, pp. 16, 26). Other conditions that SSRIs can have a role in treating are obsessive compulsive disorder and body dysmorphic disorder ((NICE 2005b), post-traumatic stress disorder (NICE 2005c, pp. 20–1), bipolar disorder (NICE 2006a, p. 9) and social phobia (Taylor, Paton & Kerwin 2007, p. 252).

The guideline for depression (NICE 2007b) says that for mild depression the options are no treatment (to see if it passes), exercise and psychological treatment. (About two-thirds of depression is categorised as mild.) For moderate depression, you should usually be offered a drug before trying psychological treatment, and this will most commonly be an SSRI. The guideline says they are as effective as other types of antidepressants, but tend to have fewer side effects. For severe depression, antidepressants and psychological treatment may be offered together. There are various options if these do not prove effective. One is to prescribe venlafaxine.

In 2007 there were 33.8 million prescriptions of antidepressants in England, of which 18.1 million were for SSRIs. There were still 10.8 million prescriptions of tricyclic and related antidepressants (Information Centre 2008, pp. 114–17). Because of their sedating properties, tricyclics may be prescribed for people with depression who also have problems sleeping, and they are sometimes used for the relief of chronic pain. They are also considered to sometimes be effective in relieving the symptoms of depression when SSRIs are not. In the USA, the number of prescriptions for all antidepressants in 2005 was 169.9 million (Stagnitti 2008, p. 1).

Neuroleptics

These drugs are also called 'antipsychotics', but this implies a greater specificity of action and use than actually applies. (The same can be said of the other drug groups, but there are not such obvious alternative names.) Neuroleptics have always been used to sedate or subdue people in institutions as much as they have been used to counter the symptoms of psychosis. The word 'neuroleptic' comes from two Greek words meaning 'seize the nerves' (see Thomas and May 2003, p. 1).

The first neuroleptic was chlorpromazine, introduced in the 1950s and marketed in the UK as Largactil and the USA as Thorazine. It is still used today. Neuroleptics are usually taken orally, but a slow-release form may be injected into a muscle. This is called a depot injection, which lasts for several weeks and may be used with people who don't otherwise take their medication regularly.

Neuroleptics are associated with some serious, disabling and highly visible adverse effects, including movement disorders, which are described later in this chapter.

In the late 1980s new neuroleptics were introduced which were called atypicals. As they have become more established they are more usually referred to as second-generation neuroleptics (SGNs). But there is no clear distinction between first- and second-generation neuroleptics. There are significant differences between drugs in each of these groups and similarities between drugs in the different groups. Generally, though, SGNs are less likely to produce the movement disorders associated with first-generation neuroleptics (FGNs), but have their own serious adverse effects including metabolic syndrome, also described later in this chapter. Clozapine is an SGN that has established a role as a drug to be used when other neuroleptics are considered to have been ineffective.

Use of SGNs grew sharply from the early 1990s, despite them being much more expensive than the older drugs. Their use was encouraged in a NICE technology appraisal (NICE 2002a), which said they should be considered for patients newly diagnosed with schizophrenia and that people on FGNs should be changed to the newer drugs if they were finding the adverse effects unacceptable. This put an end to rationing of SGNs on grounds of cost.

SGNs have been promoted with great enthusiasm by people eager to claim advances in psychiatry. For example, Louis Appleby, National Director of Mental Health for England, has written (2007, p. 7):

> As in other specialties, mental health patients are benefiting from technological advancements and new treatments. We have already seen much-needed progress in drug treatments and this is directly helping us look after patients in the community – community care cannot exist without appropriate drug therapy.
>
> Ten years ago new drugs for treating schizophrenia were being rationed. In many areas, clinicians could not prescribe above a quota that bore no relation to patient need. Patients preferred these new drugs because they do not have many of the side-effects of the older drugs, but they were considered too expensive. Since then, the use of modern anti-psychotic drugs has increased twenty-fold and they are now prescribed as a first-line treatment.

But evidence has emerged that casts doubt on the supposed superiority of the newer drugs. For example, a study funded by the NHS (Jones et al. 2006, pp. 1079–87) investigated outcomes for 227 people with diagnoses of schizophrenia or related disorders whose medication was being reviewed because of inadequate response or adverse effects. Half were prescribed FGNs and half SGNs (but not clozapine). After a year no difference was found in quality of life, symptoms or 'the adverse effect burden' between the two groups.

A serious problem of over-prescribing of neuroleptics on psychiatric wards in the UK has emerged. Guidelines stipulate maximum doses and discourage prescribing of more than one neuroleptic at a time (Taylor et al. 2007, p. 52). Yet an audit conducted by the Prescribing Observatory for Mental Health (POMH UK 2008) found that 36 per cent of patients on neuroleptics were prescribed a higher than recommended dose, 43 per cent were prescribed more than one neuroleptic and 31 per cent were prescribed FGNs and SGNs in combination. In a discussion of the audit (Paton et al. 2008), the main cause of this over-medicating was given as p.r.n. (*pro re nata*) prescribing. This is when a psychiatrist writes a prescription that allows ward staff to administer additional medication 'as required'. The authors noted (p. 438) that 'the choice of p.r.n. dose, route [oral or injection], frequency and indication may be left to the nursing staff', and drew attention to concerns that nurses may not have enough knowledge to be making these decisions.

The 2002 NICE guidance on the treatment of schizophrenia (2002b, p. 28) does not recommend psychological treatment as an alternative to drugs but does suggest it can be a useful addition: 'CBT and family work, when given with antipsychotic medication, can help reduce the number of breakdowns you have, more than just medicines alone.'

The NICE guideline on dementia (2006b) describes the role of neuroleptics. The version for members of the public first distinguishes between cognitive symptoms that affect thinking and memory, and non-cognitive symptoms that affect mood and how you behave (p. 9). It gives depression, anxiety, hallucinations, delusions, and aggressive or very agitated behaviour as examples of non-cognitive symptoms (p. 19). About neuroleptics the guidance then says (p. 12):

> If your non-cognitive symptoms are mild or moderate, you should not be offered an antipsychotic because they can have serious side effects. If you have severe symptoms (such as psychosis or you are very agitated), you may be offered an antipsychotic for a period of time, but only after your doctor has talked to you in detail about

the possible benefits and risks, which can include having a stroke or a heart attack. If you start taking an antipsychotic, it should be at a low dose at first, and your doctor should monitor you very carefully.

But according to several reports, many doctors are less cautious than they should be. In 2008, an inquiry by the All Party Parliamentary Group on Dementia concluded that around 70 per cent of prescriptions of neuroleptics for people with dementia were inappropriate, equating to around 105,000 people (BBC News 2008a).

This was followed by a survey of 355 GPs by the BBC radio programme *File on 4* (BBC News 2008b). It found more than half prescribed the neuroleptics risperidone and olanzapine to people with dementia, despite a warning from the Committee on Safety of Medicines in 2004 that they shouldn't because of the risk of strokes. The survey also found great variation in prescribing habits, with some GPs saying they would never prescribe neuroleptics to people with dementia and others prescribing them to 90 per cent of their patients with this condition.

Meanwhile, SGNs have also become established as a possible treatment for bipolar disorder, and by 2007 accounted for 70 per cent of the 6.5 million prescriptions for neuroleptics in England. There were 165,700 depot injections (Information Centre 2008, pp. 109–10). In the USA the number of prescriptions for all neuroleptics in 2005 was 24.5 million (Stagnitti 2007, p. 2).

Antimanics

Antimanics are the drugs used to control the symptoms of bipolar disorder, also known as manic depression. Antimanic drugs are also called mood stabilisers.

The most widely used is lithium. It is a naturally occurring salt and its use for a variety of medicinal purposes can be traced back to the nineteenth century and possibly even the second century (Johnson, cited in Healy 2005, p. 96). It has become established as a drug used to control mood swings since the 1960s. It may also be prescribed to people diagnosed with depression if other drugs haven't been effective. The anticonvulsant drugs, valproate, carbamazepine and lamotrigine, have been used since the 1980s. Their other main purpose is controlling epilepsy.

The NICE clinical guideline for treatment of bipolar disorder (2006a) is less directive about the use of psychiatric drugs than other guidelines for treating mental health problems. Lithium, valproate and SGNs are proposed as first-line treatments for people having a manic episode, with benzodiazepines possibly being used in addition. The same drugs, except for benzodiazepines, are also recommended for long-term treatment and there is also a role for antidepressants in treating depressive episodes. Psychological treatment may also be offered. Carbamazepine and lamotrigine are only to be used if other treatments are not successful.

In England there were 810,200 prescriptions of lithium issued in 2007 and 297,300 prescriptions of valproate, which included its use as an anticonvulsant (Information Centre 2008, pp. 110–11).

The Five Key Issues

ADVERSE EFFECTS WHILE TAKING DRUGS

The term 'adverse effects', rather than 'side effects', is used here (except when quoting from other sources) to indicate the severity of symptoms it is possible to experience. It is customary in literature about 'side effects' to refer to them as being unpleasant. Take this example from NICE guidelines, referring to neuroleptics (2002b, p. 31): 'Your doctors should keep a close eye on the side effects, as they are common and sometimes unpleasant.' The adverse effects of both FGNs and SGNs can be unpleasant, but also seriously disabling and even life-threatening. 'Side effects' is a euphemism.

When confronted with long lists of possible adverse effects it is difficult to retain a sense of proportion about them. They are a reality that has to be confronted and dealt with. But it should also be remembered that many people take drugs without experiencing any serious adverse effects. In this section the intention is not to provide comprehensive lists of adverse effects but give an idea of the type and range of effects people taking psychiatric drugs have to contend with.

Common adverse effects

These are some of the adverse effects that can be caused by most psychiatric drugs and are commonly experienced:

- sedation, drowsiness, lethargy or sleepiness can be caused by any psychiatric drug;
- the possibility of weight gain is associated with all psychiatric drugs, apart from tranquillisers (although SSRIs are more commonly associated with weight loss);

- disturbance of vision: blurred vision is associated with most psychiatric drugs and other visual disturbances can also occur, such as double vision when taking tranquillisers;
- sexual problems: the most common is loss of interest in sex, which may be accompanied by difficulties for men in having an erection and ejaculating and for women in reaching orgasm.

If these effects are minor, they may be no more than annoying; if more serious, they can have profound effects on people's lives. Sedation can cause accidents. Weight gain can jeopardise health and lower self-esteem. Visual disturbance can prevent people from reading and can lead to loss of employment. Sexual problems can cause relationships to break up.

Effects on physical health

There are many ways in which psychiatric drugs can cause serious health problems. For example, the antimanic drugs lithium and carbamazepine can interfere with thyroid function. Clozapine, olanzapine and other SGNs can cause metabolic syndrome, which is a combination of weight gain, raised cholesterol levels and diabetes. Olanzapine and clozapine are more associated with weight gain than any other prescription drugs (Dobson 2007).

Of the ten medical drugs most likely to have produced fatal reactions in patients in the period 1996–2006, four were psychiatric drugs. They were clozapine and olanzapine and the antidepressants venlafaxine and paroxetine (Lakhani 2007).

Rare but potentially fatal conditions are neuroleptic malignant syndrome and serotonin syndrome. Neuroleptic malignant syndrome is most likely to occur shortly after the person has started taking a neuroleptic. Symptoms are fever and stiffness. The symptoms of serotonin syndrome, which can occur when taking SSRIs, include jerking and twitching, tremors of the tongue and fingers, and shivering and sweating. Several symptoms need to be present for a diagnosis to be made. Both these syndromes can usually be resolved by stopping the drugs, but may require hospital treatment.

Some effects on physical health are sufficiently common and severe that patients need to have regular tests. For example, the only way of ensuring patients receive the correct dose of lithium is for them to have regular blood tests. If lithium levels become too high, toxicity occurs, causing nausea, vomiting, diarrhoea and tremor. It can cause death if not treated. People taking lithium also have to try to keep their liquid

and salt intakes even and avoid heavy sweating, as these can all interfere with lithium levels.

Movement disorders

There is a group of adverse effects known as extrapyramidal side effects
(EPS), named after part of the brain that controls movement. They are
most strongly associated with FGNs but may also be caused by SGNs
and occasionally by antidepressants, especially SSRIs. EPS include dystonia, akathisia, Parkinsonism and tardive dyskinesia:

- Dystonia is the medical name for muscle spasms, which may commonly affect the eyes, mouth and jaw.
- Akathisia is restlessness, which may be seen in compulsive movement such as pacing up and down. But it is also a mental restlessness
  which can be acutely uncomfortable and may lead to impulsive or
  aggressive behaviour.
- Parkinsonism mimics the symptoms of Parkinson's disease. Symptoms
  include muscles becoming stiff and weak and the face taking on a
  mask-like appearance. When walking the person leans forward and
  takes small steps. There can be involuntary movements and the person's mouth may hang open and produce excessive saliva.
- Tardive dyskinesia causes uncontrollable movements. They often
  start with the tongue and mouth but may spread to the rest of the
  body and may continue even after the drugs are stopped, sometimes
  for years.

Anti-Parkinson's drugs can be given to lessen the effects of EPS but
have their own set of adverse effects which may include worsening the
symptoms of psychosis.

The visible effects of EPS can look very odd and feel humiliating
and embarrassing to people who experience them. People who wit-
ness these effects may think they are signs of madness. There are also
less obvious effects, as well as akathisia, that affect the mind. They
can impair memory, ability to concentrate and capacity for abstract
thought (Krausz et al., cited in Watkins 2006, p. 62).

Other adverse effects

Other adverse effects include:

- Effects on mental health: it is unfortunate when somebody takes a
  drug for one form of mental distress and ends up with another, but it

can happen. For example, possible adverse effects of the SSRI, fluoxetine, include feeling anxious, nervous or agitated, hallucinations, mania and panic attacks.

• Paradoxical effects: these are effects which are the opposite of what is intended. Neuroleptics, for example, can make people more excited, agitated and aggressive. Tranquillisers can cause anxiety and the person taking them can become hostile and aggressive.

• Adverse interactions with other drugs: another set of adverse effects can occur when a person is taking more than one drug. So many combinations are possible that knowledge about interactions is weak. But many adverse interactions have been identified. People taking lithium, for example, are advised to avoid most painkillers. It may also interact badly with other common medicines such as steroids and drugs for high blood pressure and water retention.

• Danger in overdose: it cannot be said that any drug is completely safe in overdose, especially if taken with other drugs, but some are more dangerous than others. For example, SSRIs are much safer in overdose than older types of antidepressants.

• Effects in childbirth: psychiatric drugs can have a detrimental effect on the unborn and newly born child. Several drugs increase the possibility of foetal malformations, although the possibility of this occurring is still low. They can also affect newborn and breastfeeding babies. If the mother is taking neuroleptics, the baby may experience some of the adverse effects of these drugs; especially if she is receiving depot injections. Babies born to mothers on benzodiazepines may be born with 'floppy baby syndrome' (an absence of muscle tone) and can experience a range of other difficulties. There can be high levels of lithium in breast milk. Additionally, neuroleptics can interfere with hormones, making it harder for a woman to become pregnant.

Frequency of adverse effects associated with one drug

Table 1.1 shows the adverse effects associated with taking the SSRI citalopram (Cipramil). This is the most frequently prescribed psychiatric drug in England and there were 7.8 million prescriptions in 2007 (Information Centre 2008, p. 115).

This information (including the definitions of medical terms) is taken from the website www.medicines.org.uk. This website is managed by a not-for-profit company set up by the Association of the British Pharmaceutical Industry and funded by drug companies. Table 1.1

Table 1.1   Adverse effects of citalopram when used to treat depression in adults

Five to 20 per cent of people who take citalopram	Constipation; diarrhoea; dizziness; dry mouth; eye or eyesight problems; feeling agitated; feeling nervous; headaches; nausea; palpitations; sleepiness; sleeping problems; sweating; tremors; weakness.
One to five per cent	A drop in blood pressure on standing or sitting up; abnormal dreams; anorexia; apathy; appetite gain; concentration problems; confusion; decreased libido; ejaculation failure; faster heart rate; feeling anxious; flatulence; impotence; inability to experience an orgasm; increased salivation; indigestion; itching; memory problems; migraine; paraesthesiae (This is abnormal sensation. It can cause numbness and tingling anywhere in the body, but often in hands, feet, arms and legs); rhinitis (This is when the mucous membranes inside the nose become inflamed. Rhinitis can cause sneezing, a runny nose, and itching in the nose, throat, eyes and ears.); skin rash or rashes; stomach pain; suicide attempt; taste changes; tiredness; urinary problems; urinating more often; vomiting; weight gain or loss.
Less than one per cent	Cough; euphoria; general feeling of being unwell; increased libido; movement problems; muscle pain or tenderness; seizures; tinnitus.
Frequency unknown	Abnormal laboratory test results; aggressive behaviour; anaphylactic reactions (This is a sudden, severe, potentially life-threatening allergic reaction. The symptoms can include wheezing, difficulty breathing, rapid or weak pulse and blueness of the skin.); anger; angioedema (This is a reaction caused by an allergy. It can most commonly cause swelling around the eyes, lips, hands or feet. Occasionally it may cause swelling of the throat, tongue or lungs all of which can make breathing difficult.); bleeding problems. Blood sugar control changes in diabetics; bruising; depersonalisation (This is when someone feels they have lost their sense of reality and the world seems vague and dream-like.); feeling restless and inability to sit still; feelings of hostility; galactorrhoea (This is an abnormal discharge from the nipple. It can be milky or contain blood and it can come from one or both nipples.); gastrointestinal bleeding; hallucinations; joint pain; mania or mania-like behaviour; metabolic problems; panic attacks; photosensitivity skin reaction; serotonin syndrome; thoughts of committing suicide.

Source: Based on data taken from the Medicines Guide for citalopram hydrobromide when used for depression, accessed 20 January 2009 from www.medicines.org.uk, Datapharm Communications 2009. Medicines Guides are based on the most recently available Summary of Product Characteristics as approved by the UK regulator (MHRA).

shows the possible adverse (or side) effects of citalopram and their frequency when this information is available. A total of 74 possible adverse effects are listed. Some of them, such as serotonin syndrome, can produce a variety of different symptoms and so the number of possible symptoms is higher. Most importantly, the most harmful adverse effects tend to be the least common. If you are taking citalopram you may not experience any of these adverse effects at all, but somebody will – even the rarest and most dangerous.

CHOICE AND COMPULSION

The issue of how decisions are made about medication in mental health and who has the final say – patient or practitioner – is a fundamental one. The law provides us with some basic facts to begin with. In the UK all medical treatment, including administering medication, normally requires the informed consent of the patient or it amounts to assault or battery. To be informed, the patient needs to know what the treatment is, what it will achieve, any likely adverse effects, what will happen if the treatment is not given and what alternatives there are. Patients are also entitled to ask for a second medical opinion before deciding whether to give their consent.

But there are three sets of circumstances in which consent is not required. These are when there is an immediate danger to the patient or someone else, or when the patient is incapacitated or is detained under the Mental Health Act 1983 (which covers England and Wales).

To lack capacity to make a particular decision a person must be unable to understand, retain and weigh up information to make that decision, or be unable to communicate their decision in any way. Doctors can then decide to give treatment in the person's best interests, in accordance with the principles and legal framework of the Mental Capacity Act 2005 (which covers England and Wales). But a particular treatment cannot be given if the patient has made an 'advance decision' stating clearly that they do not want the treatment, as long as the advance decision is valid and applies to the current circumstances. However, the Mental Health Act 1983 can override an advance decision about medication.

People who have been admitted to hospital under the Mental Health Act 1983 should always be asked for their consent to treatment, but their consent is not actually required in order for medication to be given. After three months a second opinion-appointed doctor's authorisation is required if the patient refuses consent to medication or does not have capacity to give it.

All Western industrialised countries have legislation enabling the state to detain and treat people with mental health problems against their will. But powers to compulsorily treat people while they are still living in the community remain more controversial and are less universal. A recent study (Churchill et al. 2007, p. 28) found such legislation in Australia, New Zealand, Israel, most states of the USA and Scotland. Compulsory treatment in the community was included later that year in the Mental Health Act 2007 for England and Wales, which amended the Mental Health Act 1983 and came into effect in 2008.

Mental health legislation causes people who are deemed to be mentally ill to be treated quite differently from other potential patients. They can be made to take medication even when there is not an emergency and they have the capacity to refuse.

These, then, are the basic facts, but they leave a great deal of scope for interpretation. Take the issue of informed consent. What exactly should a doctor say to somebody whom they have just diagnosed as having moderate depression, for example? According to the NICE clinical guideline (2007b, pp. 23–4), 'you should normally be offered antidepressants before trying psychological treatments'. It then mentions different types of antidepressants before saying, 'your doctor will usually offer you an SSRI'. There are six SSRIs available, each with a different profile of possible adverse effects. We have already seen that one of them, citalopram, has 74 of these, even if some are grouped together. Then there are possible averse effects of withdrawal, which doctors are also expected to tell patients about. But they vary in frequency, depending on the particular drug. In the unlikely event of someone actually being given all this information by their doctor, they may be so disinclined to take any SSRI they will want to know about other antidepressants.

From one point of view that is a great deal of choice and far too much information. On the other hand, what choice is really being offered? It is a choice of taking one of a limited range of drugs. What about alternatives to antidepressants? Is the distinction between mild and moderate depression sufficiently clear-cut to justify a different set of treatment options, including whether you are first offered psychological treatment or drugs? What about the other treatments deemed suitable for people with mild depression, such as exercise, or the herbal medicine, St John's wort?

People do not only make choices when they are first offered drug treatment but also in deciding whether to continue with it. By this stage they have first-hand information at their disposal. They know about some of the effects of the treatment on them – those they can notice. Ideally they feed this information back to their doctor and, if necessary, doses are altered or drugs switched to produce better outcomes. In practice, it doesn't always work like that. Patients have a habit of making their own decisions about how they use psychiatric drugs. They stop and start them, take more or less than the proper dose and stop taking them altogether. These actions may arise from a considered decision, confusion and forgetfulness, anger and despair, or any combination of these. Whatever the motivation for not taking drugs as prescribed, this has been, to mental health professionals, 'non-compliance', which sits uneasily with the language of choice and consumerism.

Considerable concern has been expressed about mental patients – more specifically mental patients diagnosed with schizophrenia or bipolar disorder – not taking their medication. This concern has not been confined to mental health professionals and the families and friends of mental patients, but also expressed in parliament and the press. It has been based on three assumptions: drugs make people well; people who don't follow their treatment regime are acting irrationally, and this irrationality is caused by their illness. But there has been an inconsistency at the heart of these assumptions. If the drugs remove the symptoms of mental illness, then the illness cannot be influencing the mind of the person who stops taking their drugs. On the other hand, if the drugs are not working in this way, then why would the person carry on taking them?

A publication by the Medicines Partnership, *A question of choice* (Carter, Taylor & Levenson 2005), looked at the evidence of non-compliance across a range of medical conditions, the reasons for it and possible remedies. It is a difficult area to research, and figures can vary greatly from study to study, but some broad conclusions were drawn about rates of non-compliance for different conditions. Schizophrenia and bipolar disorder were considered together as 'psychotic disorders', and one figure suggested that a quarter of people prescribed neuroleptics were non-compliant. This compared with possible rates of two-thirds for people with type 2 (late onset) diabetes and people with coronary heart disease. It is suggested that people being treated for depression have the highest rates of non-compliance.

So why has there been so much concern about non-compliance by people prescribed neuroleptics? It could be because some people put themselves at risk when they experience a psychotic episode. But people with coronary heart disease risk their lives by not taking their medication, and here the link between non-compliance and death is more direct. But what distinguishes psychosis from most other medical conditions is the behaviour it can cause – behaviour that can overtly put the person at risk (more obviously than someone neglecting a heart condition), can occasionally put other people at risk and which friends, family and the public may find upsetting, disturbing and frightening.

Non-compliance by people prescribed neuroleptics became a political issue in the 1990s when a link was made between the closing down of the old mental hospitals, community care, and mental patients 'on the loose', not taking their medication and murdering people. There had been several shocking and well-publicised murders by people who were receiving or had received psychiatric treatment. But these had not become more frequent and were seldom committed by people who had stopped taking their drugs. (See, for example, Lester & Glasby 2006, pp. 34–5.) A review of homicide statistics for England and Wales for the period 1957–95 (during which most hospital closures occurred) found little fluctuation in the annual number of homicides by mentally ill people, even though the total number of homicides a year multiplied by a factor of five (Taylor & Gunn 1999, pp. 9–14). Another study showed that the majority of mentally disordered people convicted of homicide in the period 1996–9 were not acutely ill at the time and were not 'under mental healthcare' (Shaw et al. 2006, pp. 143–7). In other words, they were not being prescribed drugs. The scope for reducing homicides by forcing people living in the community to take neuroleptic drugs is limited, to say the least and, as Helen Lester and Jon Glasby wrote (2006, p. 43) before the legislation introducing supervised community treatment became law in England and Wales, 'Overall, it is difficult to see how the Draft Bill fits with the modernisation agenda of partnership working, access, and patient choice.'

The authors of the Medicines Partnership review (Carter, Taylor & Levenson 2005, pp. 7–8) suggested that effective ways of improving compliance rates involved the complementary use of educative, practical and emotionally and behaviourally supportive interventions, rather than the provision of information alone. And they say there was evidence that, regardless of the specific knowledge imparted, self-management programmes which helped to raise people's sense of effectiveness and confidence promoted better medicine taking.

But 'improving compliance rates' and 'better medicine taking' are loaded terms, especially when considering psychiatric drugs. The content of this book demonstrates that their effectiveness and safety cannot be assumed and that people prescribed psychiatric drugs are capable of making rational decisions to refuse to take them.

Perhaps a more promising approach to informed consent and good prescribing practice is to be found in the NICE clinical guideline *Medicines Adherence: Involving patients in decisions about prescribed medicines and supporting adherence* (2009a). It replaces 'compliance' with the terms 'shared decision-making' and 'adherence'. In a glossary in the full version of the guideline (NICE 2009b, pp. 31, 36) these terms are defined. Shared decision-making is described as 'a model of decision-making where information exchange is a two way process in the consultation and both deliberation and decision are made by both health care professional and patient'. Adherence, then, is 'the extent to which the patient's behaviour matches agreed recommendations from the prescriber' and 'emphasises the need for agreement and that the patient is free to decide whether or not to adhere to the prescriber's recommendation'. This contrasts with compliance, which is 'the extent to which the patient's behaviour matches the prescribers' recommendations'.

The difference between adherence and compliance may appear to be subtle, but the distinction is emphasised by one of the 'key principles' in the guideline (NICE 2009a, p. 8), which states that health-care professionals are expected to 'Accept that the patient has the right to decide not to take a medicine, even if you do not agree with the decision, as long as the patient has the capacity to make an informed decision and has been provided with the information needed to make such a decision.'

Users of mental health services are not excluded from this guideline. In fact in the full guidance (NICE 2009b, p. 50) it says: 'It is particularly important for people who are known to frequently experience inequalities in health to have their right recognised to be effectively engaged in decision-making e.g. those with learning disabilities, mental health problems and people of black and ethnic minority origin.'

This clinical guideline should bring an end to easy assumptions that users of mental health services only refuse or stop taking psychiatric drugs for irrational reasons. It also sets up an interesting tension with other NICE clinical guidelines, which can be quite firm about the benefits of treatment with drugs.

The guideline includes advice about obtaining informed consent, but this remains a challenge in mental health where there is such a range of possible adverse effects on taking and stopping medication, such a range of possible alternatives to drugs and where outcomes are so uncertain.

Critical Reflection Box 1.1

Obtaining Informed Consent

Jane was admitted to a psychiatric ward a week ago during an episode of mania. She was brought in by the police who found her running around in traffic and shouting, putting herself at risk. She is 20 years old and had no previous contact with mental health services. She agreed to stay as an informal patient and responded well to an initial combination of diazepam and olanzapine, the olanzapine being continued during the week.

She is ready for discharge and the staff team think she would be advised to continue on the olanzapine for at least another month before considering her longer-term options. She is now in a position to give informed consent and it is your responsibility to obtain it.

1. How do you introduce the topic?
2. What reasons do you give for proposing that she continues on medication?
3. What information about olanzapine should you give?
4. Do you inform her of other options?
5. How do you respond to the following comments or questions?

   - It's not going to make me fat, is it?
   - I can't think straight at the moment – you decide, you're the expert.
   - If I'm going to be on this drug for more than a few days I want to know a lot more about it. What websites do you recommend?
   - Look, I'll be fine. It was just a one-off. Anyway there's no way I'm taking that stuff any longer; it damages your brain.

PEOPLE FROM BLACK AND MINORITY ETHNIC COMMUNITIES

People from black and minority ethnic (BME) communities tend to have less positive experiences of mental health services than the majority white population. In England this was explicitly acknowledged in the 2003 report *Inside Outside* (NIMHE 2003), which was put together by a working party on behalf of the Department of Health. In her foreword welcoming the report, Jacqui Smith, then Minister of State for Health, wrote (p. 3): 'Tackling ethnic inequalities within mental health services … is one of the greatest challenges facing us. We have an obligation to meet this challenge and tackle racism and institutional discrimination within our mental health services.' The report acknowledged that use of psychiatric drugs features as one aspect of inequality (p. 13): 'Patients from all minority ethnic groups are more likely than white majority patients to be misunderstood and misdiagnosed and more likely to be prescribed drugs and ECT rather than talking treatments such as psychotherapy and counselling.'

Inside Outside was followed by another report, the *Independent Inquiry into the death of David Bennett* (Norfolk, Suffolk and Cambridgeshire Strategic Health Authority 2003). The inquiry was set up to investigate the death of an African Caribbean man who died after being restrained by nurses in the medium secure unit where he was a patient. The inquiry was also asked to contribute to the developing mental health strategy.

At the time of his death, David 'Rocky' Bennett was on three different neuroleptics (sulpiride, haloperidol and clozapine) and the antimanic, valproate. NICE guidelines (2002b, p. 16) recommend that only one neuroleptic is prescribed at a time except in exceptional circumstances. The inquiry concluded that it was unlikely that the type, dosage and combination of drugs had any significant influence on his death.

The David Bennett inquiry made several recommendations about medication that were picked up in another report, *Delivering race equality in mental health care* (Department of Health 2005). It is both an action plan based on the proposals in *Inside Outside* and also the government's response to the David Bennett inquiry. Within it are several references to providing treatment to people from BME communities which suggest there should be less reliance on psychiatric drugs. For example, the vision for 2010 (p. 4) includes: 'a more balanced range of effective therapies, such as peer support services and psychotherapeutic and counselling treatments, as well as pharmacological interventions that are culturally appropriate and effective'. But there is nothing in the report to indicate specific action to bring these changes about. Nor is there an explanation of what is meant by 'pharmacological interventions that are culturally appropriate and effective'.

Concern has been expressed about over-medication of people from BME communities and black people in particular. For example, Louis Appleby, National Director of Mental Health for England, told the David Bennett inquiry (p. 49) there was a widespread suspicion that young people from the black community tended to be treated with higher doses of individual antipsychotic drugs or with poly-medication because they were perceived by the staff to be more dangerous or more of a nuisance.

Research into ethnicity and prescribing has not focused on such a specific group as young black people and has tended to conclude that ethnicity itself is not a predictor of over-prescribing. For example, a Healthcare Commission audit of acute inpatient mental health services

(2008b, pp. 48–9) examined how many patients were given medication above recommended doses in their first week of admission and concluded that there was no significant difference in prescribing for people from BME communities and white British people.(But the conclusion is questionable – the figures in the report showed that only 1 per cent of white British people were prescribed high-dose medication for more than three days in their first week and the figure was 4 per cent for people from BME communities.) The POMH UK audit (2008) mentioned earlier in this chapter also did not find that ethnicity in itself was a predictor of over-prescribing of neuroleptics but Mental Health Act status was, and people from BME communities are more likely to be detained than white British people.

The clearest measurable difference in experience between white British people and people from some BME communities is in the proportion detained under the Mental Health Act. An analysis of service users who completed the 2005 *Survey of Users of Mental Health Services* (Healthcare Commission 2005) found that 17 per cent of the black people had been detained in the previous year compared with just 6 per cent of white British people. The figures for other minority groups were 13 per cent 'mixed', 11 per cent Asian and 14 per cent 'other' (Raleigh et al. 2007, p. 306).

A census of inpatients in mental health services in England and Wales (Healthcare Commission 2008c) found higher rates of admission than average for people from minority ethnic groups other than Chinese, Indian, Pakistani and Bangladeshi, rising to ten times the average for 'Other Black' (p. 3). Overall rates of detention were higher than average for people from these groups: Black Caribbean, Black African, Other Black and White/Black Caribbean Mixed (p. 4).

Because detention is associated with compulsory medication, people from BME communities may develop more negative attitudes towards psychiatric drugs and find themselves more often in conflict with mental health professionals. An investigation into the relationship of African and Caribbean communities to mental health services spoke of ' "circles of fear", in which staff see service users as potentially dangerous and service users perceive services as harmful' (SCMH 2002, p. 8).

Leading experts on BME mental health issues have suggested the government has undermined its own plans for improving the care and treatment of people from BME communities by introducing compulsory treatment in the community, which they fear will be used excessively to enforce compliance with medication. Professor Sashi Sashidharan, who led the working group which produced *Inside Outside*, has said (Black Mental Health UK 2007):

> It shows a lack of regard in relation to race equality. The Department of Health may say they are addressing this in policy when new law is completely at odds with it. It is a big blow and will affect the quality and care of service experience and is a significant step backwards for mental health services. The Act is a major step back for race equality and for community mental health in general.

There is another angle on BME people and psychiatric drugs which needs to be considered here. It concerns differences in the effects of drugs on people from different racial or ethnic groups. Because physical differences between racial and ethnic groups, both real and imagined, have been used to justify racism, this is a sensitive subject. But ignoring it exposes people from BME communities to risks of inappropriate prescribing.

People vary in the speed with which they metabolise drugs – we absorb them, utilise them and they pass through us. If we metabolise them slowly, they can accumulate in our bodies, causing greater adverse effects. We tend to metabolise drugs more slowly as we get older, which is why doctors should usually prescribe drugs in lower doses to older people. If we metabolise drugs more quickly than average we need higher doses to achieve the same effect.

There are differences in the average rates at which people from different racial and ethnic groups metabolise some psychiatric drugs. The examples given here, of different rates of metabolising and other different responses to psychiatric drugs, are taken from writing by Kamaldeep Bhui and colleagues (Bhui & Bhugra 1999, p. 13; Bhui & Olajide 1999, pp. 78–9):

- African Americans are at greater than average risk of lithium toxicity;
- haloperidol, a neuroleptic, is metabolised more slowly by Asian than Caucasian patients;
- clozapine-induced agranulocytosis (a potentially fatal loss of white blood cells) is more prevalent among Ashkenazi Jews than average;
- Asians metabolise the tranquilliser, diazepam, more slowly that Caucasians;
- black patients have been found to be nearly twice as likely to develop tardive dyskinesia from taking neuroleptics as white patients;

- Japanese people respond to lower levels of lithium and the neuroleptic, chlorpromazine.

And, from another source (Taylor, Paton & Kerwin 2007, p. 77): 'People of African Caribbean origin are more likely than other groups to experience clozapine-induced neutropenia – similar to agranulocytosis.'

This knowledge is patchy and needs further research. What knowledge we do have is rarely taken into account in prescribing, and people from BME communities are suffering because of it.

There is one more issue, to which Bhui draws attention. It concerns attitudes towards medication among people from BME communities. Commenting on research he carried out in London, he wrote: 'Punjabis prefer a non-medication-based approach to controlling emotions. Medication use is seen as a weakness as well as a form of intoxication of the body. Patients were reluctant to accept medication, and if they experienced any adverse effects they became absolute in their refusal to accept medication. Psychotherapeutic approaches became essential rather than optional' (Bhui & Olajide 1999, p. 12).

A belief that psychiatric drugs are basically harmful is one that is held by some people from all ethnic groups, including the white majority in Britain. But it may be more prevalent among people from BME communities and becomes another factor in their relationship to issues of choice and compliance.

Referring to the study of different 'health beliefs' among ethnic groups, Bhui and Olajide suggest that such work challenges the premise that disorders can be treated as the same and with the same treatments across all racial, ethnic and cultural groups.

THE RISE AND POSSIBLE FALL OF SSRIS

'On the appearance of any new drug an interesting cycle of events may often be observed. A trickle of favourable reports develops into a stream, and the drug becomes fashionable. Then the stream of favourable reports dries up, and accidents claim attention. The drug falls into relative disrepute, and its use may even be abandoned.' This quote is from a 1956 issue of the *British Medical Journal* (*BMJ*) and is used in a book by Charles Medawar to introduce a chapter on barbiturates (1992, p. 56). With the exception of the last phrase, it could equally have been used to describe the history of the tranquillisers which largely replaced them in the 1960s and the SSRIs which, in the 1990s, took over from tranquillisers as the drugs most prescribed for mental health problems.

The first SSRI to be licensed for use in Britain was fluoxetine, better known as Prozac – surely the best brand name for a medicine ever invented, with its evocation of positive energy. SSRIs have been described as drugs that 'resonated with the *Zeitgeist* of a generation' (Law 2006, p. 105). In the Western world, people thought they should not only not be depressed but had the right to be happy. And happiness is what Prozac and the other SSRIs appeared to offer. The manufacturers, media and medical profession colluded in persuading millions of people that their life problems had a simple explanation and a simple solution. In the USA this message was promoted through direct-to-consumer advertising and greatly aided by the publication of *Listening to Prozac* by Dr Peter D. Kramer (1993). The book cited endless examples of people whose lives had been transformed by this wonder drug, and became a bestseller. In Britain, the excitement about Prozac and its imitators was captured in a headline in the *Daily Mirror*, 'Could Fergie's pills make you happy?', followed by 'Royal rave makes Prozac a buzz word' and the disclosure that the Duchess of York and Princess Diana were both taking the drug to deal with depression and mood swings (29 April 1996, p. 24).

The way these drugs worked was described in the most simplistic terms. The public was told that the brain chemical, serotonin, controls mood; that low levels are associated with depression and that SSRIs boost serotonin levels. The myriad causes and symptoms of depression, the complexities of the brain and our ignorance about how it works were somehow swept aside.

Tranquillisers were discredited as a long-term treatment, and previous generations of antidepressants had never been particularly popular – not always effective and with a range of adverse effects patients were often not prepared to tolerate. SSRIs were claimed to be cleaner drugs with far fewer adverse effects and, unlike tranquillisers, were supposedly non-addictive.

Sales took off. By 2000 doctors in England were writing 10.4 million prescriptions a year (Department of Health 2001b, p. 115). They were boosted by the manufacturers securing licences for them to be used for a wide variety of other mental disorders, as well as depression.

But while these drugs were becoming a great commercial success, serious problems were emerging. A small percentage of people taking them experienced akathisia, a feeling of mental restlessness and agitation that can be so severe it causes people to become suicidal, violent or even murderous. Young people were especially prone to this effect. It also became apparent that SSRIs were difficult to come off. A significant proportion of people taking them experienced a quite serious withdrawal syndrome when they tried to stop. The more SSRIs were used, the more apparent it became that they were not effective for everyone to whom they were prescribed. By the time the NICE guideline for treatment of depression were issued in 2004 (2007b, p. 24), they were considered to be no more effective than other antidepressants. The guidance suggests they should usually be offered in preference to older antidepressants only because 'they usually have less side effects'.

As these problems became apparent, it was not only the reputation of the drugs that was questioned but also that of the regulators. In 2004, Richard Brook, chief executive of Mind, resigned from the MHRA's expert group on SSRIs. It had issued guidance saying that the maximum agreed dose of paroxetine was too high and should be reduced. Brook (2004) accused the MHRA of sitting on this information for a decade, saying: 'Either they didn't understand the full implications of the available medical data at the time or, worse, that data was fully understood and they failed to act. Either way it amounts to extreme negligence and a clear dereliction of the MHRA's duty to safeguard the well-being of the British public.'

Several warnings and restrictions were put on the use of SSRIs at around this time. For example, the MHRA advised doctors not to prescribe paroxetine to people under the age of 18. A subsequent investigation by the MHRA (2008) concluded that the manufacturers, GlaxoSmithKline (GSK), had withheld information that would have resulted in this advice being issued earlier. In the USA Eliot Spitzer, Attorney General for the State of New York, took out a lawsuit against GSK for withholding this information, which resulted in an out-of-court settlement of $2.5 million and GSK agreeing that in future it would publish results from all its clinical trials, positive and negative (Ethical Corporation 2004).

Meanwhile, a parliamentary committee was hearing evidence on the influence of the pharmaceutical industry. In its report (House of Commons Health Committee 2005, pp. 4, 99–101) it called for tighter controls over the industry and singled out SSRIs as an example of what can go wrong with prescribed drugs. It pointed out that although data in the original licensing application for paroxetine cited studies in which withdrawal symptoms were common, for years the MHRA maintained that they were affecting only 0.1 to 0.2 per cent of patients (one in 1000 to one in 500), before eventually acknowledging the figure to be more like 20–30 per cent. The report also used SSRIs as an example of the 'medicalisation of society' and 'a pill for every ill', saying that

'SSRIs, in particular, have been over-prescribed to individuals, often with mild forms of depression, who may be distressed by difficult life circumstances. Unhappiness is part of the spectrum of human experience, not a medical condition.'

It accused the pharmaceutical industry of 'disease-mongering', with the aim of categorising more and more people as 'abnormal' and therefore requiring drug treatment, and criticised those GPs who had prescribed SSRIs 'on a grand scale'.

Press coverage turned from stories of wonder drugs to alarm about over-prescribing. An editorial in the *Sunday Mirror* was headed 'Pills are not the cure for a nation's ills' and accused 'lazy family doctors' of doling out drugs like Prozac 'as if they were Smarties' (27 November 2005, p. 14). But doctors were expressing their own misgivings about the quantities of antidepressants they were prescribing. In a survey of GPs (Dilner 2004), eight out of ten admitted to prescribing more than they should, citing lack of alternatives, such as talking treatments, as the main reason.

But although the hype about SSRIs had subsided and serious problems with them had emerged, the number of prescriptions continued to rise, by around a million a year in England alone. Prescriptions of all SSRIs were 10.4 million in 2000 and 18.1 million in 2007 (Department of Health 2001b, p. 115; Information Centre 2008, p. 116). The only evidence of prescribing practice reflecting new doubts about SSRIs was in the near halving of paroxetine prescriptions in the same period, from 3.5 million to 1.8 million (Department of Health 2001b, p. 115; Information Centre 2008, p. 115).

The reputation of SSRIs was further dented by NICE clinical guidelines for depression and other conditions, which said that psychological treatments could sometimes be more effective (outlined earlier in this chapter). Were these guidelines to be followed, many people who would have been given tranquillisers or antidepressants could expect to be offered CBT instead. But for CBT to be readily available there was a need to train up and employ thousands of therapists. With budgets overstretched, was this really going to happen? Probably not until Lord Richard Layard, founder of the London School of Economics Centre for Economic Performance, presented a paper, *Mental Health* (Layard 2005) to a seminar at 10 Downing Street.

In his paper Layard drew attention to the amount of mental distress in Britain and the misery it causes. He proposed a major campaign against the stigma that keeps people with mental health problems marginalised and unemployed. But his masterstroke, as far as loosening the purse strings was concerned, was to point out that the government could not meet its target of getting a million people off Incapacity Benefit unless it tackled mental distress in a new way. Over a third, 38 per cent, of Incapacity Benefit claimants had a mental disorder as their primary illness and for a further 10 per cent it was a secondary illness (p. 6). And, he claimed, his proposals for making CBT and other therapies widely available would pay for themselves as people overcame mental health problems and went back to work.

The government was impressed and launched an ambitious Improving Access to Psychological Therapies (IAPT) programme for England with the intention of providing 'state-of-the-art psychological therapies for people with depression and anxiety disorders' (NIMHE 2007). (Progress of the IAPT programme can be followed at www.mhchoice.csip.org.uk.) Meanwhile, a do-it-yourself, computerised version of CBT was made available through all primary care trusts to anyone who could benefit from it and exercise and reading self-help books were being promoted as serious alternatives to medication.

It is worth noting, however, that there is some opposition to the focus on CBT to the exclusion of other forms of counselling and therapy. For example, a group of experts from the UK and USA issued a statement claiming that other forms of therapy are as effective as CBT and that the focus on CBT is limiting patient choice (BBC News 2008c).

As the programme is implemented there will be a significant change in the treatments offered to many people with mental health problems. With Health Minister, Patricia Hewitt, saying, 'Too many people are prescribed medication as a quick fix solution' (*Openmind* July/August 2006, p. 5), will sales of SSRIs and even other psychiatric drugs eventually decline?

Further grounds for limiting the use of SSRIs were provided by an examination of the research – a meta-analysis (Kirsch et al. 2008). Included in this study were results from drug company trials which were obtained using the USA Freedom of Information Act. The researchers concluded that 'There is little reason to prescribe new-generation anti-depressant medications to any but the most severely depressed patients unless alternative treatments have been ineffective.'

EFFECTIVENESS

In his foreword to the *National Service Framework* for Mental Health (Department of Health 1999, p. 1), Frank Dobson, then Secretary for State for Health, said that the standards it set for mental health services and treatments were 'founded on a solid base of evidence' which had been 'examined and validated' by the External Reference Group that produced the report. NICE makes a more modest claim, that its guidelines are 'based on the best available evidence' (NICE n.d.). The justification for any treatment intervention is effectiveness. So what is the base of evidence to demonstrate the effectiveness of psychiatric drugs?

To begin to answer this question we first have to decide what is meant by effectiveness. We know that psychiatric drugs don't cure but they can reduce or eliminate symptoms while they are being taken. So a measure of effectiveness could be the extent to which they succeed in doing that. We can take a drug and a diagnosis and ask how effective that drug is in reducing the symptoms associated with the diagnosis. The first obstacle to this approach is the weakness of diagnostic categories.

There is a rich literature criticising psychiatric diagnosis. For example, the psychologist Lucy Johnstone (2000, p. 78) is dismissive of the diagnosis of schizophrenia, saying: 'The so-called "symptoms" of the illness seem to cluster together fairly randomly, so that two people with the same diagnosis may have none in common. The diagnosis doesn't predict either the course or the outcome of the "illness", and often has no clear relationship to treatment.'

The authors of *Making Us Crazy* (Kutchins & Kirk, 1999) show how diagnoses in the Diagnostic and Statistical Manual of the American Psychiatric Association come and go according to political lobbying rather than scientific objectivity. In this way, for example, homosexuality was abolished as a mental illness and post-traumatic stress disorder introduced. Robert C. Carson (1997, p. 105), another critic of DSM, writes of 'mounting evidence that aberrant behaviors purported to be the product of underlying mental disorders are stubbornly resistant to arraying themselves into neat, tightly bounded syndromes'.

Assessments of the effectiveness of psychiatric drugs such as those by NICE assume the validity of diagnostic categories and declare whether or not particular drugs are effective treatments for people with particular diagnoses. If, as has been suggested, diagnostic categories are dubious, then the whole basis on which drugs are evaluated has to be questioned.

Challenges to the legitimacy of diagnoses come from outside the traditional institutions that determine how drugs are evaluated, but the placebo effect is accepted by all as a factor to be taken into account when assessing treatments. The placebo effect is the human characteristic of responding positively to medical and other interventions that don't have an evident biological action. People may heal from both physical conditions and mental distress simply because they believe they are being helped and expect their health to improve. The intervention may appear to be a medical treatment, such as a dummy pill they are told is a potent drug. But it may also be a human intervention, such as a doctor telling a patient that they expect them to get better. The placebo effect demonstrates a remarkable human ability to heal through the power of the mind, but one that is difficult to harness in medicine without an element of deception, raising some challenging ethical issues.

People who are sceptical of traditional and complementary medicine attribute its effectiveness to the placebo effect and the power of the relationship between practitioner and patient. Writing in 1938 (cited in Shapiro & Shapiro 1997, p. 2), when it was 'only recently that medicine has more to give', W. R. Houston suggested that the history of medicine was the history of the placebo effect, saying of doctors:

> Their skill was a skill in dealing with the emotions of men. They themselves were the therapeutic agents by which cures were effected. Their therapeutic procedures, whether they were inert or whether they were dangerous, were placebos, symbols by which their patients' faith and their own was sustained. The history of medicine is a history of the dynamic power of the relationship between doctor and patient.

Psychiatric drugs may then work on two levels, through the placebo effect and through direct biological action. To be considered legitimate drugs that can be used for medical purposes in the twenty-first century, it is necessary to demonstrate that they have some effectiveness over and above the placebo effect.

The method of measuring the effectiveness of drugs while discounting the placebo effect is called the double-blind placebo-controlled randomised controlled drug trial (RCT). The people taking part in the trial are randomly divided into two groups. One group is given a dummy pill – the placebo – and the other is given the drug being tested. Neither the people in the trial nor the researchers working with them know who has been allocated to each group (which makes it 'double-blind'). These methods are intended to eliminate bias from the trial and make it a genuine objective and scientific experiment. A positive result for the drug being tested is when the people taking it experience a greater reduction in symptoms than the people taking the placebo.

The RCT is generally seen as the 'gold standard' of research, but has its limitations. Perhaps the greatest is the difficulty in maintaining the double-blind. The placebo is nearly always an inert substance and the absence of a sensation of being on a drug means that a proportion of the people given it realise they are taking a placebo. This diminishes its power and undermines the methodology of the trial. It has been found that when a substance which produces a sensation of being drugged – an active placebo – is used, differences between results for the drug and the placebo are diminished and may disappear.

Similarly, researchers may spot who is taking a placebo because the people taking it report fewer of the adverse effects associated with the drug, which may then introduce bias into their recording of symptom reduction.

These criticisms of RCTs are taken from a study of the evidence for effectiveness of psychiatric drugs, *From Placebo to Panacea*. In this book, Seymour Fisher and Roger P. Greenberg highlight just how serious the deficiencies of RCTs are (1997, p. 370):

> two grossly different perspectives can be taken with respect to the pertinent published literature. One can accept the published find-ings at face value, except for gross and obvious defects in the design, procedure or analysis of data. However one can also justifiably take the position that all published results in this area are probably seri-ously flawed because of failures of the double-blind. Choosing the second alternative puts the investigator in the position of dismiss-ing the bulk of the work in this area and declaring that we have to deal with the hard question how one can have faith in data that has not been adequately shielded from the bias of investigators who are almost invariably highly motivated to demonstrate that given drugs are successfully therapeutic.

Joanna Moncrieff (2007, p. 21) draws attention to another major flaw in RCTs. The people who participate in them are usually already taking psychiatric drugs which they are kept on, or given a similar drug or a placebo. The people given the placebo are then at risk of experiencing a withdrawal syndrome, a factor which is generally ignored. Instead, any symptoms of distress they experience because of abrupt withdrawal are contrasted with their absence from the group who are continued on the same drug or given a similar drug, giving a falsely positive impression of the benefits of the drug relative to the placebo. (Symptoms of with-drawal in RCTs are discussed in more detail in Chapter 3.)

Evidence of the bias which these methodological weaknesses allow is demonstrated by studies of the differences in results between independent trials and those with drug company involvement. Tongeji Tungaraza and Rob Poole (2007, pp. 82–3) examined 190 published drug trials, of which 132 were RCTs. The influence of drug companies was demonstrated by their finding that 85 per cent of the RCTs were industry funded. Of the industry-funded studies, 15 per cent reported negative findings, but this rose to 36 per cent for the independently funded studies. The authors reported that this finding of bias towards more positive results in industry-funded studies was consistent with all previous studies comparing industry and independently funded trials. But they found an even greater difference when they looked at studies in which a drug company employee had participated. Only 3 per cent of these produced negative findings.

RCTs measure reductions in symptoms in the short term, usually a few weeks. But patients may take them for many years, and the short-term benefits may not last. Trevor Howard Turner (2004, pp. 1058–9) looked at long-term outcomes for people diagnosed with schizophrenia in a *BMJ* editorial, 'Long-term outcome of treating schizophrenia'. He wrote that although neuroleptics increased the proportion of people with this diagnosis who noticeably improved from 35 per cent to 49 per cent, studies suggest recovery and readmission rates are no better now than before neuroleptics were introduced. He mentions a theory that 'enhanced biological vulnerability to psychotic relapse might even be a result of the brain being made supersensitive to dopamine [a neurotransmitter], medication thus as a double-edged sword relieving the symptoms of illness but creating an increased potential for relapse once drugs are discontinued'. And he also draws attention to studies by the WHO (World Health Organization) in the 1960s and 1970s which found better outcomes for people with schizophrenia in poor countries than in rich ones. With neuroleptics being less available in poor countries, there is a possibility of the explanation being that continued use of medication correlates with poorer outcomes.

He suggests, however, that such criticisms of neuroleptics are based on 'somewhat selective viewing of the literature' and concludes that 'antipsychotics probably help but we badly need more long-term studies'.

Another review of the evidence that does exist comes to a more negative conclusion than Turner's, captured in the title of a paper 'The case against antipsychotic drugs: A 50-year record of doing more harm than good' by Robert Whitaker (2004). He proposed that the practice of maintaining schizophrenic patients on neuroleptics was not supported by evidence from research. During the period in which neuroleptics were being introduced it was possible to compare outcomes for people who were on neuroleptics with those who were not, without having to set up experiments. Whitaker referred to one such study from the 1960s of 344 patients by the USA's National Institute for Mental Health (Schooler et al., citied in Whitaker 2004, p. 6). After six weeks, there was an improvement in 75 per cent of patients treated with drugs but only in 23 per cent of placebo patients. This was taken as evidence of the efficacy of neuroleptics. But after a year patients who received the placebo were less likely to be rehospitalised than those who received drug treatment.

Whitaker also cited a quite different method of investigation, the MRI (magnetic resonance imaging) scan. One from the University of Pennsylvania found that neuroleptics caused changes in the brain associated with worsening symptoms of schizophrenia (Gur et al., 1998 cited in Whitaker 2004, p. 8).

Whitaker's summary (p. 5) concluded: 'Evidence-based care would require the selective use of antipsychotics, based on two principles: (a) no immediate neuroleptisation of first-episode patients; (b) every patient stabilized on neuroleptics should be given an opportunity to gradually withdraw from them. This model would dramatically increase recovery rates and decrease the percentage of patients who become chronically ill.'

When considering the effectiveness of psychiatric drugs it is relevant to compare them with alternative interventions. There are alternatives, which are claimed to be viable, to all psychiatric drugs, including neuroleptics. The publication *Recent Advances in Understanding Mental Illness and Psychotic Experiences* (British Psychological Society, 2000) made the case for using CBT and other psychological therapies with people diagnosed with schizophrenia. For example, it cited studies showing that CBT can help people to positively change their attitudes towards delusional beliefs.

Loren Mosher, the psychiatrist who set up the experimental Soteria House, conducted research which showed that patients treated without drugs were less likely to relapse and more likely to be well-functioning after two years than patients receiving conventional treatment. (For more information on Mosher and Soteria House visit http:// moshersoteria.com/.)

After reviewing, with others, evidence about the effectiveness of all psychiatric drugs, the editors of *From Placebo to Panacea* wrote (Fisher & Greenberg 1997, p. 371): 'Are we suggesting that psychoactive drugs do not work? No, that is not our message. Although such drugs probably often do not work much better than active placebos, many troubled individuals likely have benefited from them.' But they suggest that such benefit does not necessarily stem from particular chemical actions but more from the process and ritual of taking them (p. 372):

> in some conglomerate way, different factors unite to impact apparent therapeutic power to the act of an authority figure administering a psychoactive substance to troubled individuals. The complex of ingesting a substance that palpably induces 'druglike' body experiences, in the context of personally feeling the need to change or improve, and the added element of receiving authoritative reassurance that now there is a good probability of changing – all seem to offer an opportunity for a therapeutic process to be set in motion.

Their most succinct summary of the evidence on effectiveness is this (p. 381): 'no one is in a confident position to tell patients how effective psychoactive drugs really are'.

Discussions of effectiveness rarely include consideration of adverse effects. One reason for this was captured in a *BMJ* editorial by Jan P. Vandenbroucke, a professor of clinical epidemiology (2004, pp. 2–3). He argued that whereas measures of effectiveness rely almost exclusively on RCTs, research into adverse effects is predominantly through observational studies such as using large databases that link routine prescriptions with the occurrence of unexpected disease. He suggested that 'The protagonists of these fields barely know each other: they publish in different journals, write and read different books, and work in different departments. They are even suspicious of each other's methods.'

His dream is for them to learn from each other and work more closely together to 'marry the best evidence on benefits with the best evidence on harm in a single balanced review to assist doctors and benefit patients'.

Each person experiences different combinations of benefits and harm and will have a unique take on them depending on their own values and tolerance of different symptoms. Fewer panic attacks but no orgasms; threatening voices subdued but a greater risk of heart disease; less fear but less joy in life. This is the reality of the choices people make, if given a choice, about whether or not to take or stay on psychiatric drugs. It is this reality which is examined in detail in the next chapter and which adds so much to our understanding of the role of medication as the dominant treatment in mental health services. Like studies of benefits and harm, studies of people's experiences and views of psychiatric drugs tend to be another separate area of activity. In Chapter 2, I integrate them into the discussions of the five key issues begun here and so link them with the scientific evidence, official guidelines and policies, current practice and criticisms of these by professionals that I have included in this chapter.

Critical Reflection Box 1.2

Effectiveness

1. Having read this section are you more or less convinced of the effectiveness of psychiatric drugs? Why?
2. You are in charge of devising the best ever research project for determining how effective one type of psychiatric drug is and have an unlimited budget. Describe it. What are its strength and weaknesses? What are the ethical considerations?

Service-user views in overall helpfulness

3. In Chapter 2 there is a table listing different groups and types of psychiatric drugs in the order service users rated them for overall helpfulness in one survey. Try listing these groups of drugs in the order you expect them to appear in the table and write something about why: antidepressants, antimanics, neuroleptics, tranquillisers.
4. Do you expect FGNs or SGNs to be rated most highly? Why?
5. Do you expect SSRI or tricyclic and related antidepressants to be rated most highly? Why?

2

What People Taking Psychiatric Drugs Have to Say about Them

I have been on over 30 antidepressants in over 37 years. I have had to take many courses of ECT because no helpful drug could be found. Now I think I have found it.

I wasted a year of my life on this drug. I was a zombie.

These two quotations, taken from a survey by the Scottish Association for Mental Health (SAMH 2004, pp. 47–8), immediately demonstrate the contribution that service users can make to our understanding of psychiatric drugs. Both people were talking about the same drug, the antidepressant venlafaxine (Efexor). The literature about psychiatric drugs tends to focus on their global effects – whether overall a drug is better than a placebo, better than another drug, and so on – whereas surveys of service users' experiences and views remind us of the wide variation in people's individual responses to psychiatric drugs.

This SAMH survey, published as *"All you need to know?"* in 2004 was the most comprehensive study of the service-user experience of psychiatric drugs to date. It was based on 756 completed questionnaires from people living in Scotland who had received a new or different prescription in the previous three years. Two other surveys, published around the same time, also generated new data and insights about the experience of being prescribed psychiatric drugs.

Also in 2004, the Healthcare Commission (which became the Care Quality Commission in 2009) began a series of annual surveys of service users' views of community mental health services in England, the *Survey of Users of Mental Health Services* (2004). It was certainly the biggest survey of its kind, with over 27,000 people completing questionnaires. Although people were not asked for their views on psychiatric drugs, it did inquire about process – how involved they were in decisions concerning their medication and how much information they were given about adverse effects. Through being repeated annually it promised to demonstrate whether service users really were becoming more involved in decisions about treatments.

A year later Mind published a report of its survey *Coping with Coming Off* (Read 2005), which was the most in-depth exploration of people's experiences of deciding and trying to come off psychiatric drugs. Interviews with 204 people produced qualitative as well as quantitative data which gave revealing insights into relationships between people who prescribe psychiatric drugs and monitor their use and the people who take them but may wish to stop. A comprehensive account of the findings of this survey is presented in Chapters 4, 5 and 6.

Coping with Coming Off (CWCO) was one of a series of surveys carried out by Mind which began with a collaboration in 1983 with *That's Life!*, a BBC TV consumer and entertainment programme hosted by Esther Rantzen, after it featured the stories of three people who felt they had become hooked on tranquillisers. The controversy about whether these widely prescribed drugs were addictive had been around for years, but featuring it on such a popular TV programme brought it a new prominence and provided a focus for many people who were struggling with these drugs on their own. The show received 3000 letters from people who had taken tranquillisers and Mind produced a questionnaire which was eventually completed by 2170 of them. The report was published as *That's Life! survey on tranquillisers* (Lacey & Woodward 1985).

Until this time, the drug companies, regulatory bodies and medical establishment had largely succeeded in covering up the serious problems associated with these drugs, despite the efforts of courageous dissident doctors and researchers. (There is a detailed account in Medawar 1992.) Patients who reacted badly when they stopped taking tranquillisers were usually told by their doctors that the drugs were not addictive. The disturbing sensations they experienced when trying to cut down or stop were, they were told, the symptoms of anxiety or depression returning, demonstrating that they needed to stay on the drugs.

The *That's Life!* survey demonstrated, beyond dispute, that patients were being misled by their doctors. It showed that the drugs were being prescribed carelessly and for too long; that the adverse effects could be worse than the original distress the drugs were intended to treat and that getting off them could be a nightmare.

All this was possible because a television programme gave those who were receiving this treatment a collective voice – a way of speaking up outside the confines of a doctor's surgery. Singly, they could be ignored.

Their perceived status as neurotic, anxious people undermined their credibility as chroniclers of their own condition. But together, they commanded attention.

In the mid-1980s, organisations such as Survivors Speak Out and the United Kingdom Advocacy Network were yet to make their mark. The rhetoric of 'user involvement' was some years off. And yet, for the first time, people who were receiving psychiatric treatment were able to substantially influence the delivery of that treatment. The survey was one aspect. Dedicated volunteers – often people who had successfully struggled to come off minor tranquillisers themselves – formed self-help groups for others trying to do the same, and these groups were often also active in publicising the dangers of tranquillisers. There were plenty of people willing to talk to the press, and a medical scandal makes a good story. Faced with a torrent of bad publicity, the regulatory bodies and the medical profession responded by setting strict limits on the prescribing of tranquillisers.

The impact of this survey demonstrates the value of asking people who have taken psychiatric drugs to talk about their experiences and perceptions of treatment. It led to a succession of other reports which form the basis of this chapter. It also illustrated some of the strengths and weaknesses of surveys as a research method. There is a limitation to any piece of research where the people who contribute are volunteers who have made some effort to be included in the research. It is fair to assume that the experiences of people who responded to the *That's Life!* questionnaire were not completely typical of people who had been pre-scribed tranquillisers. We can, of course, be equally sure that we don't know what a more typical or representative group would be. We can speculate that people who had a hard time on these drugs had more incentive to write in to the programme and then fill in and return the questionnaire than people who were content with their treatment – but we just don't know.

The statistics from all these surveys should be treated with caution, but not ignored. In the *That's Life!* survey 2000 people had tried to come off their tranquillisers. Of these, 1500 reported that it had been difficult and over 1000 said it was very difficult. Such a statistic has to be a powerful indicator that not all is well. What bring these statistics to life are the personal accounts. Between them, these stories and sta-tistics paint a vivid picture of what went wrong when doctors didn't listen to and respect their patients.

The *That's Life!* survey was not only significant for having contrib-uted to the uncovering of a major piece of medical malpractice. It was also the first time the views of people diagnosed as mentally ill had been sought, recorded and publicised in this way. Previously, they had been observed, measured and asked to self-assess their symptoms. But once diagnosed with a mental illness, even of the so-called 'neurotic' variety, they were deemed to be too lacking in judgement and objectivity to have valid views about their treatment. But no one could read these accounts by people with the lived experience of taking tranquillisers and honestly claim they lacked validity.

As a direct result of the success of the *That's Life!* survey, Mind devised another research project that would be even more challenging to traditional views about the credibility of people diagnosed as mentally ill. The People First survey, published as *Experiencing Psychiatry: Users' Views of Services* (Rogers, Pilgrim & Lacey 1993), sought out the experiences and views of people who had at least one inpatient admission. The majority of people who took part were diagnosed with schizophrenia or manic depression; people with even less status and credibility than those who contributed to the *That's Life!* survey.

Since then, there have been a succession of other surveys which have deepened our knowledge and understanding of what it is like to take psychiatric drugs. Mind has published two surveys on the adverse effects of drugs (Campbell, Cobb & Darton, 1998; Cobb, Darton & Juttla, 2001). Rethink (formerly the National Schizophrenia Fellowship) has published several reports with an emphasis on taking neuroleptics based on results from a survey of 2222 people who had taken psychiatric drugs and some focus groups (NSF n.d.(a), (b); Rethink 2006). A research project by the Mental Health Foundation, *Knowing Our Own Minds* (MHF 1997), covered not just treatments and services but also the ways people find to live with and overcome mental distress.

These surveys each cover all or some of the countries that make up the UK. They were initiated by voluntary-sector organisations which, generally, have been ahead of statutory services in recognising the contribution of service users. They are about giving people an opportunity to express their opinions and the possibility of influencing policy and practice.

Survey of Users of Mental Health Services, the annual Healthcare Commission survey, has a different purpose. It is to see how well providers of mental health services are doing in achieving targets intended to produce better services. In one respect it is methodologically superior to the other surveys in that people are randomly selected to take part. But, as only about a third respond – 35 per cent in the 2008 survey (Healthcare Commission 2008a) – much of this advantage is lost. It has value but, unlike the other surveys, does not draw on the reflections and perceptions of service users. In an article entitled 'Form of Torment' the novelist and service user, Clare Allen, has written about her frustrations in trying to fit complex experiences into simple choices of tick-boxes (Allen 2007).

Another significant survey from a statutory organisation, the Mental Health Act Commission, was *Count Me In: The National Mental Health and Ethnicity Census 2005 Service User Survey* (MHAC 2005). The aim of this survey was to provide information to support implementation of the action plan, *Delivering Race Equality* (Department of Health 2005). There were two parts to it: a census of inpatients by ethnicity, and interviews with inpatients to compare the experience of BME inpatients with that of other inpatients. Since then the census has been repeated annually, but not the interviews.

Put together, all this work gives us a great deal of useful and relevant information about people's experiences of psychiatric drugs which can be used to re-examine the key issues identified in Chapter 1 from the patients' perspective.

The Five Key Issues

ADVERSE EFFECTS WHILE TAKING DRUGS

> *I don't know what is going on most of the time. I walk strangely, lack energy and feel sick when I take lithium.* (Campbell, Cobb & Darton 1998, p. 10)

> *I was given haloperidol, it made my limbs stiff. It gave me anxiety, I was suicidal.* (Cobb, Darton & Juttla 2001, p. 12)

These descriptions of being on the antimanic drug, lithium, and haloperidol, an FGN, bring to life lists of adverse effects and demonstrate how difficult it can be to live on psychiatric drugs.

In some respects, people taking them are best placed to describe and evaluate adverse effects. In other ways their perspective may be limited. When you are feeling bad it can be difficult to disentangle the effects of the drug, symptoms of the distress it is intended to alleviate and other unrelated feelings and ailments. This may cause people to discount adverse drug effects. Additionally Peter Breggin (2006, p. 201), a critic of psychiatric drugs, has proposed that they have a 'spellbinding' effect which, he explains: 'causes the victim to underestimate the degree of drug-induced mental impairment, to deny the harmful role that the drug plays in the person's altered state, and in many cases compels the individual to mistakenly believe that he or she is functioning better'.

Another limitation of self-observation is that people on medication are not necessarily aware of long-term health problems which may be developing. As always, the service-user perspective is essential to the knowledge base but doesn't replace other lines of research and inquiry.

Two surveys showed significant differences in the proportion of people taking a psychiatric drug or drugs who reported experiencing adverse effects. The figure from *"All you need to know?"* (SAMH 2004, p. 89) was 61 per cent, whereas 92 per cent of participants in the Rethink (Rethink 2006, p. 5) survey reported an adverse effect. This difference may be explained by the questions they asked. In *"All you need to know?"* respondents were asked if they had experienced unwanted effects when taking a drug. In the Rethink survey they were prompted by being asked which, if any, of seven common adverse effects they experienced, as well as being offered another category of 'other'.

Table 2.1 shows the frequency with which people in the *"All you need to know?"* survey reported adverse effects from different drug groups. The drug groups associated with the highest incidence of adverse effects – neuroleptics and antimanics – are those which people more often stay on for long periods and are most likely to be compelled to take under mental health legislation.

A closer look at the data (p. 89) enables us to see if adverse effects were less common with modern drugs compared with the older drugs they are tending to replace. In fact the frequency was quite similar. Of people taking SSRIs 59 per cent experienced at least one adverse effect and the figure for people on tricyclic and related antidepressants was 54 per cent. Of people taking SGNs, 66 per cent experienced at least one adverse effect and the figure for people taking FGNs was 70 per cent.

Table 2.1 The frequency of adverse effects when taking psychiatric drugs

Drug group	No. in group	Those experiencing adverse effects (%)*
All neuroleptics	541	68
All antimanics	170	64
All antidepressants	728	58
All tranquillisers	81	36
All drugs	*1520*	*61*

* In all tables percentages have been rounded up or down to the nearest whole number.

Source: Data taken from *"All you need to know?"* (SAMH 2004, p. 89).

There were, however, significant differences between specific drugs. For example, the antidepressant with the highest frequency of adverse effects was the SSRI, paroxetine, with 75 per cent. Lofepramine, a tricyclic, had the lowest frequency with 43 per cent (p. 50). For neuroleptics, the drug with the highest frequency of adverse effects was the FGN, haloperidol, with 85 per cent. Amisulpride, an SGN, had the lowest frequency, with 59 per cent (p. 71). (Results for drugs taken by fewer than 20 people are not included.)

Mind's research into people's experiences of adverse effects told us which were the most common across all psychiatric drugs. Most frequently mentioned was weight gain, followed by muscle shaking/tremor, loss of energy/lethargy and feeling sick/nausea (Cobb, Darton & Juttla 2001, p. 10).

Rethink asked people who had taken a variety of psychiatric drugs to rate adverse effects as tolerable, bad or very bad. The adverse effects with the highest proportion of people who experienced them saying they were very bad were 'other' (38 per cent), sexual side effects (31 per cent) and weight gain (30 per cent) (NSF n.d.(a), p. 5).

Adverse effects can be extreme but some people will put up with a great deal if there are compensatory benefits. This was demonstrated in *"All you need to know?"* (SAMH 2004, p. 20), which listed some of the comments on adverse effects of lithium made by people who still rated it as a very helpful drug. They included:

> *I pile on weight. I have a permanent tremor and often have double vision.*

> *Bloated feelings, dry mouth, increased weight gain. Slowed down physical movements, trouble getting up in the morning.*

> *Loss of thyroid function; polyuria; polydipsia.*

Polydipsia is excessive thirst, and polyuria involves producing large quantities of urine. Both are linked to diabetes. Despite the disabling adverse effects, these people still valued lithium highly for the way it controlled their symptoms.

It is, perhaps, harder to identify and measure how drugs interfere with ability to think and feel, rather than the physical effects. It comes across more strongly in quotes than statistics. One person wrote about antimanics (MHF 1997, p. 40):

> *I find lithium (and carbamazepine) hamper one's ability to think normally. Between episodes I prefer to do without. That way there is more joy*

in my life. The drugs leave you without feeling and (it is) very difficult to be in touch with one's inner self.

Someone who had taken the SSRI, citalopram, wrote (SAMH 2004, p. 31)

I felt it made me worse; I felt dead inside. No interest in life, stayed indoors, summer and autumn, until I finally came off it.

This quote is from someone who participated in a focus group on the adverse effects of neuroleptics (Rethink 2006, p. 7):

You can't feel like normal people feel, you can't feel your emotions properly. Yeah, it dampens you and that's not nice because you can't feel happy and you can't feel sad, you're just like a zombie kind of thing.

Adverse effects have an impact on the quality of people's lives. Rethink found that 33 per cent of people on neuroleptics said lack of concentration and tiredness caused by medication affected their ability to carry out daily activities. A quarter (25 per cent) had lost their motivation to do things and 25 per cent also talked about the stigma of sounding or looking odd owing to speech and movement difficulties (Rethink 2006, p. 7).

Many people who take psychiatric drugs seem to swap one set of symptoms for another. The symptoms of their mental distress may be subdued but replaced with a set of adverse effects that amount to a general feeling of being unwell. This interferes with their ability and motivation to pursue activities that can help their sense of emotional well-being: exercise, eating well, socialising, hobbies, work. This may be one explanation of why success in symptom relief doesn't always translate into successful long-term outcomes.

There are possibilities for minimising adverse effects if patients are given good information so they can identify them and report back, and doctors listen and are prepared to adjust doses and try different drugs or alternative approaches. Research suggests there is room for improvement.

The 2008 Healthcare Commission national survey asked people who had been newly prescribed medication in the last 12 months whether they were told about the possible side effects. Only 40 per cent said 'yes, definitely', 28 per cent said 'to some extent' and 32 per cent said 'no' (Healthcare Commission 2008a, tables section C). Deciding what information to give people, when and in what form, is not a simple matter, but surely it is possible to improve on these figures.

Doctors are not always helpful when people raise concerns about adverse effects. In Mind's research only 29 per cent said their doctor was helpful (Campbell, Cobb & Darton 1998, p. 13). A woman with a diagnosis of schizophrenia told Rethink that she approached her GP for advice about the weight she had gained after changing to a new neuroleptic. She was informed that at her age, her appearance was of little consequence and that no doubt she would not be looking for a partner (Rethink 2006, p. 4). In contrast, one person in the *"All you need to know?"* survey (SAMH 2004, p. 13) reported

> *My GP was excellent and makes time available to discuss everything to ensure I am OK with things.*

Research into service users' experiences of adverse effects shows that they can have a significant negative impact on their lives and are sometimes intolerable. Newer drugs are not necessarily associated with fewer adverse effects but there are significant differences in the frequency of adverse effects between different drugs of the same type.

There is room for improvement in doctors' communication about adverse effects and their ability to listen to and respond to feedback from service users. Perhaps this difficulty suggests there is scope for other mental health workers, especially those who have a role in administering and monitoring medication, to become more involved in information giving and negotiating about what drugs, if any, people should be taking.

CHOICE AND COMPULSION

We have already seen how people frequently lack the information to give informed consent to treatment with psychiatric drugs. Evidence from surveys also demonstrates how seldom people feel they have been given a real choice about whether to take drugs at all, about which drug to take or about alternatives to drugs.

People responding to the *"All you need to know?"* survey were asked about their most recent prescription, and only 50 per cent were very or fairly happy it had been a joint decision (SAMH 2004, p. 11). From the Healthcare Commission survey, we find that only 44 per cent said they definitely had a say in decisions about their medication (Healthcare Commission 2008a, tables section C). People may feel that decisions about medication are out of their hands, even if legally, they are not. One person told Rethink (Rethink 2006, p. 9):

> *You can suggest that you want to change your medication but at the end of the day it's their decision.*

Mind's second report on adverse effects included these contrasting experiences (Cobb, Darton & Juttla 2001, p. 22):

> *I have been stable for some time and would like the opportunity to try to reduce my dose, which I was promised, but now they have gone back on it.*

> *I asked if I could go into hospital for a rest. I refused all drugs. I asked for counselling and it got me well again.*

In this report Mind listed the choices about medication people said they wanted (p. 22). They included:

- changing to a different drug;
- more expensive drugs to be made available to all (since this survey was published the more expensive SGNs are no longer rationed on grounds of cost);
- use of the lowest possible dose;
- 'holidays' from drugs or a drug-free 'window' to see how you are doing;
- shorter periods on drugs;
- choice based on information from the patient's and others' experiences;
- a choice of alternative treatments such as talking treatments, crisis centres and the opportunity to self-manage;
- a choice about whether to have treatment at all.

One person (p. 22) wanted:

> *Just to be free of medication the rest of my life.*

These desires suggest a more collaborative and equal relationship with doctors than many people experience, with a more holistic approach to treatment and less emphasis on psychiatric drugs. Such desires are consistent with initiatives described in the introduction and Chapter 1, such as the recovery approach, shared decision-making and adherence and NICE guidelines recommending psychological therapies.

When people are not offered the choice they want, one option is to take things into their own hands and stop taking their medication. One person told Rethink (NSF n.d. (b), p. 6):

> *I suffered in silence until I could take no more. In the end I became non-compliant and ended up in hospital.*

Others are more successful. For *"All you need to know?"* (SAMH 2004, p. 190), one person wrote:

> *I'm now off Seroxat. It was pure hell but I done it. I will never take it again. They were not pleased about me not wanting to take it.*

In the Rethink survey 42 per cent said they had, at some point, stopped taking their medication without the knowledge or support of their doctor. Adverse effects of drugs was the reason most often given for wanting to come off them (Rethink n.d. (b), p. 6).

We have seen, using the example of lithium, that people may be prepared to put up with serious adverse effects if they are balanced out by sufficient benefits. But if they do not perceive the advantages to outweigh the disadvantages they want to have their concerns taken seriously and the option of changing medication or trying another approach. But people don't always feel able to raise their concerns and, if they do, may find they are not taken seriously. It is perhaps not surprising, then, that some people make their own decisions to stop taking their drugs.

Many service users in England were against extending compulsory powers to people living in the community. Research about service-user groups (Wallcraft, Read & Sweeney 2003, p. 46) found that their members were generally opposed to it on the grounds that it would lead to more oppressive services, worsen relationships between professionals and service users and should not be necessary if the right services are in place. Service users are perhaps getting a mixed message from the government and Department of Health; being offered the prospect of more choice in some respects but less in others.

PEOPLE FROM BLACK AND MINORITY ETHNIC COMMUNITIES

There are four surveys (in addition to CWCO) which included sufficient numbers of BME people to be able to produce some meaningful figures. Mind's second survey on side effects (Cobb, Darton & Juttla

2001) included responses from 82 BME people out of a total of 502 (16 per cent). For the *Count Me In: Service User Survey* (MHAC 2005) 200 BME inpatients out of a total of 394 (51 per cent) were interviewed. Sixty (15 per cent) people who responded to the *Knowing Our Own Minds* survey (MHF 1997) were African Caribbean. On a different scale altogether is the Healthcare Commission's annual *Survey of Users of Mental Health Services*. The 2004 and 2005 surveys (Healthcare Commission 2004, 2005) were analysed according to ethnicity. In the 2005 survey 10 per cent of the 25,000 people interviewed were from BME communities (Raleigh et al., 2007, p. 305).

Additional information comes from a recording of a meeting of a group of black people (of African and Asian heritage) who were service users at the same mental health trust (Black service user group 2000).

Some of the struggles experienced by people from BME communities are expressed by a black woman responding to the Mind survey on side effects:

> *The attitude of doctors that they will not listen/respect what the patient says about side effects, wrong dosage, etc., makes it hard to trust them and put your faith in their ability to get it right. This means I see them as the enemy – not really helping me. They see my attitude as proof of my illness and so they press to increase my medication. I feel they create a situation where I can't win. I am therefore forced to take things into my own hands and I do it fairly well! I do not relapse.* (Cobb, Darton & Juttla 2001, p. 16)

With the exception of the Healthcare Commission survey these surveys indicate that people from BME communities have worse experiences of psychiatric drugs than other people. For example, two surveys show them having more limited choices. In the second Mind survey on adverse effects only 17 per cent of people from BME communities said they had been offered a choice of treatment compared with 28 per cent of the rest. In *Knowing Our Own Minds* 75 per cent of the white people but only 45 per cent of the African Caribbean people had experienced talking treatments (MHF 1997, p. 63).

The following exchange among a group of African and Asian heritage service users illustrates how they perceived racism in a psychiatric hospital and its impact on medication issues:

R: *Have you ever been to the pharmacy to ask them about your medication? That's really important because the doctors have such an attitude that they don't really talk to you.*

M: *They think you're nothing.*

R: *Even with drugs, they don't say 'let's put you on antidepressants', they don't recognise depression in black people. It's either an antipsychotic or a mood stabiliser.*

T: *That's right, it's true. They check us as aggressive and when you get on mood stabilisers, all you can do is sleep, eat and sleep.*

M: *Everyone in the hospital is seen as rebellious. Because we've got attitude about us, when we kick off or when we just talk about things, they don't like it, they don't appreciate it.* (Black service user group 2000)

The *Count Me In Service User Survey* asked inpatients various questions that related to their experience of taking psychiatric drugs. Before presenting the figures an explanation of the categories used is required. 'White' includes all white people including, for example, Irish people who are sometimes regarded as a minority ethnic group. 'Black' is used for people who identified as Caribbean, African, black British and similar. The other categories were 'mixed', 'Asian' and 'other'. They have been combined here and called 'other minority ethnic'.

Nearly a third (31 per cent) of white people said they had been offered a choice of medication, but this figure fell to 20 per cent for people from other minority ethnic communities and 19 per cent for black people. Three-fifths (60 per cent) of white people said their treatment plan had been well explained on admission, but this figure fell to 52 per cent for people from other minority ethnic communities and 41 per cent for black people (MHAC 2005, p. 19).

This pattern of white people giving the highest rating followed by people from other minority ethnic communities and then black people was repeated throughout the survey, including in responses to a series of questions about psychiatrists and nursing staff such as how polite, friendly and honest they were. One of these questions was 'Do psychiatrists or nursing staff listen to what you have to say?' The responses are shown in Tables 2.2 and 2.3 and have relevance to communication about medication.

Table 2.2   How often psychiatrists listen to what service users have to say (%)

	No.	Always	Sometimes	Rarely or never
White	187	59	29	12
Other minority ethnic	120	50	34	16
Black	69	39	39	22

Table 2.3   How often nursing staff listen to what service users have to say (%)

	No.	Always	Sometimes	Rarely or never
White	192	55	36	9
Other minority ethnic	121	49	45	7
Black	73	36	40	25

Source: Data for Tables 2.2 and 2.3 taken from *Count Me In: The National Mental Health and Ethnicity Census 2005 Service User Survey* (MHAC 2005, pp. 23–4).

Critical Reflection Box 2.1

Noticing, Thinking about and Taking Action against Discrimination

1. Think of a time you have experienced, observed or heard about an incident in which someone or some people were discriminated against on grounds of ethnic or racial identity. What was it, why do you think it happened and how did it make you feel? If you were personally involved, did you try to stop it or not? How did that feel?
2. Think of the mental health service, project or team you are most familiar with. What evidence is there of it taking action to provide a service that is equally valued by people from all racial and ethnic groups? How well do you think it is doing and why? What is one way it could be doing better?

In contrast to the *Count Me In* survey, analysis of the *Survey of Users of Mental Health Services* (Healthcare Commission 2004; 2005) found little variation in experiences between white British people and people from BME communities (Raleigh et al. 2007, pp. 304–12). The sophisticated analysis factored out differences between white British people and people from BME communities that were not about ethnicity. For example, being detained in hospital resulted in a more negative experience, and the figures were adjusted to exclude this variable so that it didn't confuse the comparison based just on ethnicity. This is a legitimate form of analysis but, as the figures from this survey in Chapter 1 demonstrate, people from BME communities were more likely to have been detained and therefore had negative experiences for that reason. It would have been helpful if this paper had shown unadjusted as well as adjusted figures.

Overall, figures from all these surveys confirm the consensus that people from BME communities experience discrimination in mental health services and that this includes more negative experiences of being prescribed medication. They also show that people from different minority ethnic groups may have different experiences.

THE RISE AND POSSIBLE FALL OF SSRIS

In October 2002 the BBC TV programme, *Panorama*, broadcast 'Secrets of Seroxat'. It alleged that paroxetine (Seroxat in the UK, Paxil in the USA) could make people self-harm and provoke suicide and violence, and raised concerns that it might be addictive. Following the programme, 67,000 people phoned the BBC helpline and nearly 1400 emailed *Panorama* with their thoughts. In May 2003 the BBC followed up with 'Seroxat: E-mails from the Edge', which examined the accounts of people who had emailed.

There were disturbing echoes of the *That's Life!* survey of nearly 20 years previously. Once again, there were stories of drugs being handed out too readily, of patients not being believed by their doctors and people feeling alone as they struggled to get off them. Once more, a drug company was shown to be covering up and a regulatory body to be negligent. And again there were also people writing in, distressed by the criticism, to say that taking Seroxat was the best thing that ever happened to them.

As with *That's Life!*, *Panorama* was not saying anything new. There were researchers and doctors who had uncovered the problems with this drug and been speaking out for some time. Patients had been communicating with and supporting each other through the internet. But the combination of a high-profile TV programme and the testimony of people taking the drug brought these concerns into the mainstream.

In 'Secrets of Seroxat', *Panorama* reported a legal case from the USA where a man who had taken just two paroxetine pills murdered his wife, daughter and granddaughter before killing himself. The manufacturers, GlaxoSmithKline, blamed his depression for the murders, but the jury concluded that it was paroxetine that provoked this man into a killing spree. Many people who emailed *Panorama* did not believe this could be true. But among the emails were accounts of 16 suicides, 42 serious suicide attempts and 92 cases of people having serious thoughts of harming themselves or others. One man wrote (Panorama 2003):

> *On the day of taking Seroxat I woke up, and my temperature inside my head felt really hot. As the day progressed it got worse and worse until in the evening it felt like the inside of my skull was boiling. I went to bed and I started thinking that everybody was out to get me. I started to feel angry, murderous, I wanted to kill my partner and my family. I've never felt like that before. I sat on the edge of the bed holding my knees up against me because I knew that if I moved I would kill everybody.*

The parallels with *That's Life!* and tranquillisers were not exact. Unlike tranquillisers, SSRIs do not stop working after a few months. And *Panorama* concentrated on one drug rather than a class of drugs. Although all SSRIs can induce the same destructive adverse effects and be difficult to come off, paroxetine appears to be the worst. In *"All you need to know?"* it was the SSRI most likely to produce adverse effects while being taken and on stopping. It was also the lowest scoring SSRI for helpfulness, with 28 per cent rating it as very unhelpful (SAMH 2004, pp. 29, 32, 34). But SSRIs in general were not rated highly by respondents to the *"All you need to know?"* survey. Table 2.4, later in this chapter, shows them being rated as less helpful than the tricyclic anti-depressants and tranquillisers they have largely replaced.

Undoubtedly people have benefited from SSRIs. One person wrote about citalopram (SAMH 2004, p. 34):

> *There is no doubt in my mind about this medicine; taking it has given me back my life.*

SSRIs offer another choice, a different spectrum of benefits and harms from other drugs. But the evidence which comes directly from people taking them supports other research which shows that they do not represent some kind of breakthrough. On merit, they should not have achieved such a dominant position as a treatment for mental health problems.

EFFECTIVENESS

How do people who take psychiatric drugs weigh up their effectiveness? For a few it is simple. There are people who derive tremendous benefit from taking them. Their distressing symptoms clear up and any adverse effects are minimal. They may be able to stop taking the drugs or be happy to stay on them, feeling the drugs are giving them a quality of life they could only otherwise dream of. They may be aware of possible long-term effects on health, but feel it is well worth taking the risk. For others, the opposite applies. Their drugs have little if any positive affect on symptoms or even make them worse. And the adverse effects are so severe they can barely function. If they try to come off them and run into further difficulties, their negative experience is compounded.

The quotes at the beginning of this chapter demonstrate how these extremes can be experienced by different people taking the same drug.

The following quotes show people having equally contrasting experiences of FGNs:

> *Calming effect, quick acting, no side effects, pleased to take it.*

> *I felt I had no positive effects from the drug, only side effects.*

The first drug was sulpiride and the second chlorpromazine (SAMH 2004, pp. 61–2). But most people are more ambivalent, as captured by these comments, also about chlorpromazine (SAMH 2004, p. 61):

> *It did work a treat – like blotting paper absorbing all the emotions – but overall I was not happy.*

> *It did some positive things while on a psychiatric ward, but I hated it.*

Perhaps speaking for everyone who takes their medication reluctantly, another wrote of the same drug (SAMH 2004, p. 67):

> *Damned if you do, damned if you don't.*

Often, nothing is very clear-cut. Someone may start taking a drug during a crisis and be grateful for its initial impact. Years later they are unable to work; they attend a day centre with the occasional spell in hospital and wonder what happened to their life. This person, interviewed for the CWCO research, captured the confusion people may feel:

> *I just wish there could have been two of me – one took the road without Seroxat and one took the road with Seroxat. 'cos I want to know if Seroxat has had a positive influence on my life or if it's been a burden. That's the thing that interests me. I don't know if it's held me back all these years and if I would have been at a better stage if I never took the drug in the first place.*

Although it is not always easy to answer a question about how helpful your drug is, we can get some kind of measure from the summary of findings from *"All you need to know?"* shown in Table 2.4. It shows how people rated drugs overall for helpfulness, taking into account both positive and negative effects.

If we cover up the column on the right we are left with a table in which the responses 'very helpful' and 'fairly helpful' have been amalgamated, as have 'fairly unhelpful' and 'very unhelpful', and 'neither' has been excluded. At first glance, psychiatric drugs come out of this

Table 2.4 The helpfulness of psychiatric drugs

	No.	Rated unhelpful or very unhelpful (%)	Rated helpful or very helpful (%)	Rated very helpful (%)
All tranquillisers	*83*	*17*	*77*	*44*
All antimanics	*167*	*17*	*69*	*35*
SGNs	287	23	66	35
All neuroleptics	*535*	*26*	*62*	*32*
Tricyclic and related antidepressants	141	21	63	30
FGNs	209	26	61	28
All antidepressants	*722*	*25*	*56*	*24*
SSRI antidepressants	364	29	54	21
Other antidepressants	86	28	44	21
Depot neuroleptics	39	43	38	21
All drugs	*1505*	*24*	*61*	*28*

Source: Data taken from *"All you need to know?"* (SAMH 2004, p. 89).

well. For each drug group – antimanics, neuroleptics, tranquillisers and antidepressants – more than twice as many people rate them helpful as rate them as unhelpful. For antimanics and tranquillisers, the proportion is considerably higher. Some of this positive experience will have come from the placebo effect and, in one sense, should be discounted, were it possible to calculate. But of course people in this survey are not comparing a drug with a placebo and are not necessarily going to care how any benefit is obtained.

What is reasonable to expect from a psychiatric drug? For many people it is their only treatment. They hope the drug will be decisive in reducing their symptoms, will produce no adverse effects or tolerable ones and be safe. If these expectations are met they are bound to say it is very helpful. Look at the column on the right of the table. If we take these to be the 'satisfied customers', then they are in a minority, less than one in three, taking all the drugs together. Even people who vote 'very helpful' are not necessarily having a wholly positive experience. As we saw in the section on adverse effects, some people will put up with harmful effects from their medication if they are balanced by effective relief of symptoms, and still rate their drug 'very helpful', but it is hardly ideal.

It is interesting to see tranquillisers being rated as the most helpful type of drug, especially as they were strongly criticised in the *That's*

Life! survey 20 years previously. Since then restrictions have been put on their use and this may actually account for their popularity. People use them continuously for short periods or from time to time as needed. The usual conflicts over compliance do not occur. Instead, people self-medicate, which may be a more popular way of using psychiatric drugs. This is more possible with tranquillisers because they have a fairly instantaneous effect unlike, for example, antidepressants, which may take up to two weeks before any beneficial effects are felt. It is worth noting, though, that not everyone has a positive experience of these drugs. These comments illustrate different responses to the anxiolytic diazepam (Valium) (SAMH 2004, pp. 81–2):

> *Valium is the most 'instant relief of tension' tablet I have ever taken.*

> *I spent most of the eight weeks I took this drug either vomiting or sleeping! I was covered in bruises and couldn't continue to function.*

In the *"All you need to know?"* survey depot injections were considered separately from neuroleptics taken orally and received lower ratings. In fact, they were the drugs considered to be least helpful, and the only type of drug that more people rated unhelpful than helpful. This replicates results from Mind's first survey on adverse effects. The experience of 124 people on depots was compared with that of other people on psychiatric drugs. It was found that they were less likely to have been given enough information and warned about adverse effects, less likely to have found their doctor helpful, and less likely to have found their medication helpful overall (Campbell, Cobb & Darton 1998, p. 14).

In contrast to tranquillisers, compliance is central to the way depot medication is used. The long-acting injections and regular appointments are intended to ensure that people remain under their influence continuously and for long periods of time. The justification for their use has to be that people they are given to would be significantly worse off without them; so why do the majority of them disagree? Presumably staff who prescribe and administer depots have a different view, but have failed to communicate it convincingly. The experience of the majority of people on depot injections appears to encompass the worst aspects of the use of psychiatric drugs. But, as always, people have a wide range of responses, as these comments illustrate (SAMH 2004, p. 68):

> *It reduced voices in my head and intrusive thoughts.*

> *Slept 20 hours a day and was suicidal for a year.*

As with adverse effects, there were bigger differences in ratings of individual drugs rather than between different types of drugs. Ratings of very helpful for different types of antidepressants ranged from 30 per cent for tricyclic and related to 21 per cent for SSRIs and other. The antidepressant with the highest positive rating was the tricyclic-related drug, trazodone, with 40 per cent rating it as very helpful (p. 40), and the lowest rated was the SSRI, paroxetine, with only 15 per cent finding it very helpful (p. 24). Similarly, SGNs were rated as very helpful by 35 per cent and FGNs by 28 per cent. But the highest and lowest ratings both went to FGNs. Sulpiride was rated as very helpful by 46 per cent, whereas zuclopenthixol only scored 14 per cent (p. 66). The different antimanic drugs were similarly rated for being very helpful, but lithium received less negative ratings than did the anticonvulsants that are used as antimanics, valproate and carbamazepine (p. 78).

We can gain another perspective on effectiveness by comparing how people rate drugs relative to other treatments. The various forms of counselling and psychotherapy – talking treatments – are possible alternatives to psychiatric drugs, and there are some data that compare people's evaluation of them to drug treatment. There are also data on electroconvulsive therapy (ECT), still used as a second-line treatment for depression.

Knowing Our Own Minds (MHF 1997) gives us figures for the proportion of people who found a variety of treatments and activities helpful or helpful at times. They have been collated to form Table 2.5.

Table 2.5 The helpfulness of treatments or activities

Treatment or activity	No.	Helpful or helpful at times (%)
Hobbies and leisure activities	209	97
Talking treatments	280	88
Art and creative therapies	162	85
Physical therapies	144	85
Exercise and postural therapies	116	85
Antidepressants	263	67
Dietary and natural supplements	102	63
Neuroleptics	236	55
ECT	107	30

Source: Table compiled from data taken from MHF 1997.

Another set of evaluations of non-medical approaches comes from the Rethink report *A Question of Choice*. Of people who had received talking treatments, 79 per cent rated them helpful or very helpful. Cognitive behavioural therapy was rated separately from other talking treatments at 72 per cent, nutritional/diet scored 70 per cent, art/music 81 per cent, homeopathy/herbal 61 per cent, exercise 85 per cent and training/education also 85 per cent (NSF n.d. a, p. 6).

A report from Mind, *Ecotherapy: The green agenda for mental health* (2007, p. 1). promoted the value of green exercise and included a survey of people who participated in a variety of mental health projects such as gardening and walking in the countryside. It found that 94 per cent of the people taking part thought the activity was beneficial to their mental health.

Another source of data about talking treatments is the Healthcare Commission survey. Of the people who had received talking treatments on the NHS, 52 per cent said it was definitely useful and 33 per cent said it was useful to some extent. People were not asked if they thought their drugs were useful, so a comparison cannot be made (Healthcare Commission 2008a, tables section D).

We can conclude from these surveys that most non-medical approaches are evaluated as more helpful than drugs. But expectations come into it. Whereas people may expect drugs to provide some kind of cure and may have the same expectation of talking treatments, they may not consider an activity such as pursuing a hobby or leisure interest in the same way. A hobby might earn a 'very helpful' rating for lifting someone's mood for a few hours whereas therapy might have to achieve more to be rated as very helpful. But this look at a wide range of approaches does suggest that there are many routes to regaining mental health and the more we include, the better our chances of success. The *Knowing Our Own Minds* research also showed that people could benefit from religious and spiritual beliefs and personal and self-help coping strategies, but didn't attempt to quantity their helpfulness.

A further comparison comes from a survey of members of the Manic Depression Fellowship, now known as MDF The BiPolar Organisation (Hill, Hardy & Shepherd 1996, pp. 33, 46). People with this diagnosis were asked what had been of most benefit to them since the onset of their illness. Rated highest were family and friends, chosen by 33 per cent, followed by drug treatment, chosen by 25 per cent. Carers were asked what had been of most benefit to the person they cared for and 60 per cent rated drug treatment as the most useful factor. It is interesting to see such a disparity in the results. It supports the notion that sometimes drug treatment may suit others (family, professionals, the wider community) better than it suits the people actually taking them. Another interpretation is that people close to the person taking drugs see the benefits (perhaps a less chaotic and risky life) more than they see the adverse effects (feeling less alive, the physical ailments), or value the balance between the two differently. Some people with the diagnosis of manic depression or bipolar disorder have written about what they miss when they learn to control their mood swings even though they may feel they benefit overall (see, for example, Kimish 2001). Similarly, others value aspects of their minds and lives that are regarded as symptoms of mental illness, such as hearing voices (see, for example, Romme & Escher 1993), or see 'madness' as a necessary process they must experience and move through rather than have subdued with medication (see, for example, Russo 2001).

This evidence of effectiveness from surveys of people who have taken psychiatric drugs offers a different perspective from other research. It shows that people more often find psychiatric drugs helpful rather than unhelpful, but only a minority find them very helpful. The range of responses to medication is wide, with different people taking the same drug having a range of experiences from the very positive to the very negative. Talking treatments are rated more highly than drugs, as are many other approaches to improving mental health.

This wide variation in response to psychiatric drugs, the absence of evidence to demonstrate the superiority of newer drugs over older ones and the significant differences in adverse effects associated with different drugs of the same type all point to the importance of finding the best drug for each person through a process of experiment and discussion between patient and doctor.

So far we have looked at guidelines, clinical practice and people's experiences of taking psychiatric drugs. But also of significance is what happens when they try to stop taking them. The process of deciding if and when it is appropriate to stop medication, the question of whether psychiatric drugs are addictive and guidelines for good practice in withdrawing are fraught with controversy, muddle and uncertainty. These issues are thoroughly examined in the next chapter.

Critical Reflection Box 2.2

Service User Perspectives on Effectiveness

1. In Critical Reflection Box 1.2 you were invited to anticipate some findings that appear in Table 2.4. How did you do? If the findings are different from what you expected, see if you can find explanations in this chapter.
2. Table 2.4 shows that respondents to *"All you need to know?"* were more than twice as likely to rate psychiatric drugs as helpful than as unhelpful. But less than a third rated them as very helpful. In the comment on this table it is suggested that the second figure is more significant. What are your thoughts about it?
3. In Table 2.5 and the text that follows a range of activities and approaches to improving mental health are rated as significantly more helpful than psychiatric drugs. But is suggested that, with the exception of talking treatments, they may not have to achieve as much as psychiatric drugs to be rated as helpful. Is this fair? What are your thoughts about it?
4. Are your views about psychiatric drugs challenged or confirmed by this chapter? If they are challenged, how convinced are you by the evidence presented here?

3

What is Known about
Coming off Psychiatric Drugs

Introduction

We have already seen how staying on or coming off psychiatric drugs can become a battleground between doctors and patients. At their most extreme, disputes are resolved by the law. Medical staff are empowered to literally force medication on their patients. Even when this power is not used, knowledge of it lurks in the background as a threat hanging over the reluctant recipient, turning negotiation into an uneven contest.

But patients have their own source of power and control. For the majority, taking their medication is a private, unsupervised act. They can decide not to. Even inpatients can avoid medication by becoming adept at pretence – tucking pills under their tongues until they are out of sight of nurses. We have seen in Chapter 1 that non-compliance is commonplace, though no more so than among patients taking long-term medication for physical health conditions.

For people on psychiatric drugs non-compliance may be an act of defiance arising from a desperate desire to be free of some life-ruining adverse effect or effects, whatever the risk. It may be a cool, calculated decision to carefully withdraw without alarming mental health professionals. It may be less deliberate, arising from forgetfulness, confusion or a haphazard lifestyle. It can be any combination of these.

Other decisions about stopping are taken more co-operatively. Patient and doctor may agree that the balance of wanted and unwanted effects is such that a drug should be stopped, even if only to try another. They may even agree that the drug has worked and the patient should be fine without it, although this is a complex issue, which we will discuss in more detail later on. These easier negotiations and agreements are more likely to occur in GP practices than psychiatrists' offices. In primary care, mental health legislation is a more distant threat or responsibility and people tend to be more entrusted with their own care. Roles may even be reversed, with GPs attempting, without success, to persuade patients who have been on tranquillisers for years to give them up, but reluctant to use their authority to refuse prescriptions.

In this chapter we examine guidelines for the circumstances in which people should stop taking psychiatric drugs, we look at what is known about the process of coming off them and we consider the long-term consequences of staying on and coming off medication.

The Decision to Try Coming off Psychiatric Drugs

This introduction has given some of the reasons why people, with or without their doctors, decide to stop taking psychiatric drugs. Next we look at what official guidelines and expert opinion have to say about how long drugs should be taken for and what should prompt a decision to come off them.

TRANQUILLISERS

There are clear guidelines which doctors are expected to make patients aware of when they first prescribe tranquillisers. The NICE guideline on treating generalised anxiety disorder (2007a, p. 22) says: 'If you are offered benzodiazepines, they should be used only for a maximum of 2–4 weeks as the beneficial effects wear off over a longer period. Using them for longer also increases the risk of dependence and the likelihood of withdrawal effects when the time comes to stop taking them.' There is similar guidance for use of Z-drugs (NICE 2004a, pp. 6–7).

But the *Panorama* survey (2001) described in Chapter 1 – whose research estimated that around a million people in Britain had been prescribed tranquillisers for more than four months since guidance was first issued in 1988 – suggested that there was a startling discrepancy between policy and practice and produced this memorable exchange between presenter Shelley Jofre and National Director for Mental Health, Louis Appleby:

Jofre: *The guidelines that were introduced in 1988 were very clear. They said benzodiazepines shouldn't be prescribed for more than four weeks at a time. Which part do you think doctors didn't understand?*

Appleby: *I think the guidelines are completely clear. I don't think there's any problem in understanding them. I think the problem has been that changing individual prescribing practice requires more than guidelines. It's also necessary for doctors to have a clear idea of what alternative treatments there are, meaning different drug treatments but also in particular meaning psychological therapies for anxiety.*

Jofre: *Isn't that their job to know what sorts of treatments are available?*

Appleby: *Yes, yes it is, but prescribing practice changes slowly and I suppose that's one of the lessons of this whole disaster.*

This TV programme was not followed by any new initiative to limit prescribing of tranquillisers or to offer assistance and support to people wanting to get off them.

ANTIDEPRESSANTS

NICE guidance on the treatment of depression (2007b, p. 27) has this to say about how long people should stay on antidepressants: 'You should be advised to take antidepressants for at least 6 months after you feel better because this reduces the risk of your depression coming back. Your doctor should check to see if you need to stay on medication after this.'

Similar guidance is given for staying on antidepressants used for other purposes. The key phrase here is 'feel better'. Of course, some people don't feel better because they are taking an antidepressant. For example, in the *"All you need to know?"* survey (SAMH 2004, p. 34), which provided much of the material for Chapter 2, only 54 per cent of people taking an SSRI said it was helpful. Presumably the rest should stop taking it, not because they feel better but because they don't feel better. Some people will feel somewhat better but not free of depression. They may then want to stay on the drug for the limited benefit they feel they are experiencing. People who find the drug very helpful (21 per cent of people on SSRIs in the SAMH survey) may be fearful of coming off a drug that has been so effective. Interpreting the guideline in practice is not straightforward.

An indication of the difficulties people may have in deciding to stop taking antidepressants comes from two GP practices in Shropshire: Church Stretton and Bishop's Castle. In 2005, an audit identified people who had been taking SSRIs for more than 18 months, had been well for more than six months and were at low risk of relapse (Quayle et al.,

2008). They were invited to come off their medication with the support of a community psychiatric nurse (CPN). As a result, 59 patients went on to come off their drugs or start to reduce them. These people clearly fulfilled the criteria in the NICE guideline but did not stop taking their drugs until they were offered some additional encouragement and support. If this pattern is repeated across the UK, with an estimated 10,147 GP practices (figure supplied by Royal College of General Practitioners), there are nearly 300,000 people taking SSRIs unnecessarily and who could potentially come off them.

Evidently there are doctors who don't accept the NICE guideline. Responding to the launch of Mind's *Coping with Coming off* report (Read 2005), Dr Sarah Jarvis, representing the Royal College of General Practitioners, said on Channel 4 News (11 September 2005):

> *If somebody wants to come off an antidepressant they should certainly talk about it with their GP and then the GP can work in partnership with them. But we have to accept that mental health, that depression, is very much an illness, in the same way as diabetes is. If I have a patient that I start on a diabetes or a blood pressure tablet they don't expect to come off it a few years later. They know that it's important for them to stay on it.*

A rather different view is expressed by Joseph Glenmullen (2005, p. 105), a psychiatrist who has written several books about antidepressants: 'Taking antidepressants for years, even decades, is an ongoing human experiment which should not be undertaken lightly.'

NEUROLEPTICS AND ANTIMANICS

NICE guidance on treating schizophrenia (2002b, p. 23) has this to say about stopping neuroleptics: 'Generally, it's better to keep taking antipsychotics for 1 or 2 years after your last breakdown.'

They are also one of several drugs which may be used in the long-term treatment of bipolar disorder. NICE guidance on the treatment of bipolar disorder (NICE 2006a, p. 13) says:

> Long-term treatment varies from person to person, but it usually continues for at least 2 years after an episode and sometimes up to 5 years. During this time your doctor should see you regularly. If you wish to stop taking medication within this time, you should discuss this with your doctor. If, after discussing advantages and

disadvantages with your doctor, you decide not to take medication long-term, you should still be offered regular appointments.

It is interesting to note that NICE guidance suggests that, after a period of stability, people with diagnoses of schizophrenia and bipolar disorder can expect to discontinue their medication. This position is a direct challenge to the chemical imbalance/drugs-for-life stance so often taken by psychiatrists. What it means in practice is difficult to say. If doctor and patient both believe the patient owes their stability to the drugs, they may be reluctant to tinker with what they see as a successful regime. If either is sceptical, then it offers encouragement to experiment. 'Defensive prescribing' occurs when doctors keep people on drugs because they fear criticism if they stop the drugs and something goes wrong. These guidelines perhaps permit a more adventurous approach. From the patient's perspective they offer something to aim for and can be used to challenge mental health staff if they are resistant to proposals for reducing or coming off medication.

The Experience of Trying to Come off Psychiatric Drugs

Potentially, there are adverse effects involved in coming off or reducing the dose of any psychiatric drug. The reason why is well explained by John Watkins (2006, p. 360):

> Prolonged and continuous exposure to neuroleptics or other drugs which have powerful effects on the central nervous system causes the brain to adapt to their constant presence. When the drugs are stopped or the dose is substantially reduced, the brain's equilibrium is temporarily upset and a process of readjustment must occur as the brain gradually gets used to functioning without them. Since the initial adaptation may have taken many weeks or months, the readjustment process may require a similar length of time, possibly even longer.

It is this process of adjustment that causes symptoms of withdrawal. Like the adverse effects of taking drugs, they are not predictable and can cover a vast range. There are various ways of organising lists of possible symptoms. In the report of the *Coping with Coming Off* research

(Read 2005, p. 6) the following categories were chosen:

- emotional problems, such as mood swings, depression and anxiety;
- cognitive problems which are about using the mind, such as difficulty concentrating and memory loss;
- symptoms associated with psychosis, such as hallucinations and paranoia;
- physical problems, such as headaches, digestive complaints and difficulties with balance; and
- sleep disturbance, such as nightmares and sleeplessness.

People often report 'flu-like symptoms' which cover several of these categories.

Disputes arise about the language used to describe these symptoms and the reasons for them because of what it implies about the nature of these drugs.

In the 1980s, doctors and drug companies had to admit that tranquillisers possessed similar characteristics to illegal drugs of addiction, although they preferred to use the word dependence. Their justification for this distinction was that people were not getting hooked on them through recreational abuse. The distinction could be dismissed as a euphemism designed to cover up the dangers of tranquillisers, but it is one that was welcomed by many of the people struggling to get off them and who didn't want to be called addicts, a term they associated with illegal activities, degenerate lifestyles and an element of choice in having deliberately taken drugs known to be addictive. Others, however, embraced the term 'addict' as a way of drawing attention to the harm caused to them by the medical profession.

According to the 1980 edition of the *Diagnostic and Statistical Manual of Mental Disorders* of the American Psychiatric Association (DSM-III), either tolerance or withdrawal effects were a sign of dependence. Tolerance occurs when someone needs greater quantities of a drug to achieve the same effect. Subsequently it became widely accepted that tranquillisers are associated with both withdrawal effects and tolerance, doubly qualifying as drugs of dependence under this definition (Social Audit 2003).

It cannot be coincidence that for the 1994 edition, DSM-IV, the definition of dependence was radically changed to exclude tranquillisers. The new definition of dependence which was retained for an updated version published in 2000 required three or more of the following to be present:

- tolerance;
- withdrawal effects;
- the substance is often taken in larger amounts over a longer period than was intended;
- persistent desire or repeated unsuccessful effort to cut down or control substance use;
- a great deal of time is spent in activities necessary to obtain the substance, use of the substance, or recover from its effects;
- important social, occupational or recreational activities have been given up or reduced because of substance abuse;
- continued substance use despite knowledge of having had a persistent or recurrent physical or psychological problem that was likely to have been caused or exacerbated by the substance. (Abbreviated from American Psychiatric Association 2000, p. 197.)

Glenmullen (2005, p. 23) gives an explicit account of how the drug company, Eli Lilly, went about creating a linguistic term to distance its SSRI fluoxetine (Prozac) from language associated with drug dependence. Eli Lilly paid for a group of psychiatrists to meet and discuss growing concerns about difficulties people were having withdrawing from this drug. From this meeting came a proposal to avoid using the term 'withdrawal' and refer instead to a 'discontinuation syndrome'. After the meeting Eli Lilly paid them to write eight papers on antidepressant discontinuation syndrome which they sent out, free of charge, to doctors to help establish the term.

Withdrawal symptoms can occur when coming off any psychiatric drug, although they vary in their frequency and severity. But just as people respond very differently to taking psychiatric drugs, they can have different experiences of coming off them. One person can have a massive struggle over a long period to get off a psychiatric drug while another stops taking it with no difficulty at all.

The factors that influence dependence on drugs, whether they are prescription, social or illegal, are complex and not entirely understood. Environmental factors appear to play a part, as is illustrated by experiments with rats. In the 1960s and 1970s the addictive power of morphine (the medical name for heroin) was apparently demonstrated by showing that rats were so attracted to it that they would subject themselves to pain and even starve to death in order to obtain continuous access to the drug. But one psychologist, Bruce Alexander, noted that these sociable creatures were kept isolated in cages with nothing to stimulate them. In 1981 he and colleagues built an attractive and environment for rats which he called 'Rat Park' in which the rats lived together. They showed no interest in morphine at all. Rats that already appeared to be addicted to morphine lost interest in it when they were moved to Rat Park, even though they would have been expected to have developed a craving which they could easily satisfy. (Information about Rat Park is taken from Slater 2004, pp. 157–81.)

Rat Park suggests that, as with the effects of taking psychiatric drugs, withdrawal effects are not simply caused by the chemical action of a drug on a brain.

Expectations of success or failure can influence outcomes on coming off, just as they influence outcomes while on drugs. Joanna Moncrieff (2006, p. 3) uses the term 'nocebo effect' to describe the inverse of the placebo effect. She suggests that the nocebo effect can produce a negative outcome if the person coming off the drug or people involved in their care do not expect them to succeed.

Staff who have been taught that people with diagnoses such as bipolar disorder and schizophrenia have to stay on medication for life will obviously be liable to worry about them stopping or even reducing their drugs and may not expect them to succeed. This was illustrated in a small study of staff reactions to 10 patients on a long-stay ward who had been stable on neuroleptics for a year and were being prepared for discharge (Thomas, Katsabouris & Bouras 1997, pp. 692–4). The ward team decided to try to find the lowest dose of medication on which these patients could remain stable. Doses were successfully reduced over six months, with just one increase for one patient. Meanwhile it was noted by the researchers that some key workers had negative attitudes towards the reduction plans and these attitudes persisted even though patients' mental states and behaviour didn't change. They recorded that 'On several occasions minor behavioural manifestations such as "the patient not getting up on time" or "refusing to attend activities" were interpreted as possible relapses.'

Patients themselves can fear coming off medication, and David Healy (2005, p. 157) suggests this fear can develop into a phobia. People who develop this response can benefit from psychological support. It follows that someone who is encouraged to approach withdrawal with confidence, provided they are also well informed about the possible adverse effects and the best ways of managing them, may well have an improved chance of succeeding.

The usual recommended method of withdrawing from a drug while minimising possible adverse effects involves coming off it gradually. Drugs take different lengths of time to pass through the body and there are significant variations even among drugs of the same type. The 'half-life' of a drug is the average time it takes for the quantity in the person's blood to drop by half. Drugs with short half-lives are sometimes associated with more frequent withdrawal symptoms than those with longer ones. This can be counteracted by coming off especially slowly or by switching to a similar drug with a longer half-life. (Information about the half-lives of different drugs can be found in Appendix 2.)

One suggestion for coming off gradually, or tapering, is to reduce in steps of 10 per cent of the original dose at a time but to reduce in smaller steps towards the end. (See, for example, Breggin & Cohen 1999, pp. 137–8.) Tapering is made easier if the drug is available in low doses and, even better, available in liquid form. Then, using a dropper, dosage can be graduated by tiny amounts. Again, it might be worth switching drugs to be on one that is available as a liquid. (Information about minimum available doses and drugs available in liquid form is included in Mind's pamphlet *Making Sense of Coming off Psychiatric Drugs*. Details of this and other sources of practical information can be found in Appendix 1.)

If someone, for whatever reason, decides to come off drugs without involving their doctor, they are deprived of opportunities to follow some of these practical steps. Changing from one drug to another, swapping from pills to liquid or lowering the strength of the pills you take cannot easily be done without a doctor's co-operation.

The great confusion about coming off drugs occurs when withdrawal symptoms are mistaken for signs of the distress for which the drugs were first prescribed. This may be taken as evidence that the person needs to go back on their medication and proof that they cannot manage without it. This unfortunate and unnecessary sequence of events is especially likely if there is no knowledge or acknowledgement of withdrawal symptoms. But even when there is, there is still scope for confusion. David Healy suggests three ways of distinguishing between withdrawal symptoms and 'new illness episodes' when coming off neuroleptics or SSRIs:

1. If symptoms arise within hours, days or even weeks of discontinuing treatment, it is likely evidence of a dependence syndrome rather than a new episode of distress. If the person has come off their drugs

while well it should be several months before a new psychotic or affective episode appears.

2. If the symptoms clear up quickly on resuming treatment, this should be taken as an indication of a dependence syndrome unless it can be proved otherwise.

3. If the pattern of symptoms is somewhat different to the initial pattern of symptoms the person had before starting treatment, this is also a good indicator of a dependence syndrome. (Based on Healy 2005, pp. 258–9)

If the information presented here is acted upon, someone attempting to come off their drugs should stand a significantly better chance of a successful outcome than someone who is unaware of what they might be letting themselves in for. But there are some other factors that come into play which are more about attitude than simply following good practice guidelines. It must help if the person coming off the drug feels in control of what they are doing and has some confidence in their ability to succeed, both in getting off and staying off. Being in control may be about initiating or agreeing with a decision to come off. It may be about following a tapering programme but at a speed which makes sense for the person doing it. Confidence may come from having a positive vision of life without drugs, a belief such as 'I'm better now, I don't need them' or 'there are better ways of dealing with my distress'. For some people feeling in control will be about finding out everything there is to know about what they might face. For others, that would be overwhelming. The challenge for mental health workers is to provide the right amount of information, support, warning and reassurance for each person.

Getting off psychiatric drugs can be about more than dealing with symptoms that arise directly from the process of eliminating them from the body, especially if the person has been on them a long time. Drugs may act as a buffer between them, the world and even their own emotions. As they adjust to life without them, everything can seem louder, brighter and rawer than before. Information about coming off drugs (given in the resources listed in Appendix 1) is as much about how people can prepare for life without them as identifying and coping with withdrawal symptoms.

The information provided so far applies to coming off any psychiatric drug, but there are differences in what can be expected that depend on the type of drug being withdrawn from.

TRANQUILLISERS

Given the caution with which tranquillisers are now supposed to be prescribed it may come as a surprise to learn that many people who take them for long periods do not become dependent. One source estimates it to be one-third (Ferguson 2005, p. 22). But although many people do not find it difficult to come off them, they are still recognised as being drugs of dependence. NICE guidelines (2007a, p. 36) even mention the word addiction: 'Benzodiazepines have a substantial risk of addiction and can cause withdrawal problems.'

This is because they are not only associated with withdrawal symptoms, but people become tolerant to them quickly and so they meet a definition of dependence that requires both tolerance and withdrawal. Additionally they are drugs of abuse, traded illegally and snorted or injected.

No list of possible symptoms of withdrawal is exactly the same. Brian Ferguson's (2005, p. 24) has the advantage of distinguishing between common and rarer symptoms. He lists common symptoms as anxiety, depression and panic symptoms such as palpitations, sweating, tremor, nausea, hyperventilation, headache and tension. Rarer symptoms are nightmares, seizures, psychosis, perceptual disturbances such as perceptual ataxia, and hypersensitivity to noise and other sensations. Perceptual ataxia is a feeling of being uncoordinated and unbalanced. David Healy (2005, p. 155) lists other possible symptoms, including numbness, muscle pains, restlessness, abnormal taste and gastrointestinal cramps, as well as the ubiquitous flu-like symptoms.

People taking these drugs for the correct amount of time can still experience withdrawal symptoms if they stop abruptly. The patient information leaflet which comes with the hypnotic, temazepam, suggests tapering even after taking it for four weeks. Withdrawal symptoms can start within 24 hours of stopping or reducing a short-acting tranquilliser or sleeping pill but may take several days to emerge if the drug is longer acting. Diazepam is the longest-acting benzodiazepine, with a half-life of one to four days. Switching to diazepam and then tapering is a possible strategy for people having trouble coming off a shorter-acting drug. It is available in liquid form (as are some other benzodiazepines), which allows for more gradual tapering.

Symptoms generally last up to six weeks, but for a small minority they may last much longer. Ferguson (2005, p. 25) suggests that if patients are supported through withdrawal by their GPs, success rates can be 80–90 per cent. He also notes that once coming off the drugs has been raised by a doctor, many people choose to do it in one go. People who struggle to come off can be assisted by self-help groups and through learning non-pharmaceutical methods to manage anxiety, such as physical relaxation methods.

ANTIDEPRESSANTS

The presence of a withdrawal syndrome for SSRIs and similar antidepressants such as venlafaxine is now beyond dispute. But there are still differing versions of how frequently it occurs and the severity of the symptoms. These differences are marked out by the language used to describe what may happen when people stop taking these drugs. NICE guidelines (2007b, pp. 29–30) have this to say:

> you should be told that, although antidepressants are not addictive, in the way alcohol and cigarettes can be, you might experience unpleasant symptoms when you stop the medication, miss doses or reduce the dose of the medication. These symptoms are referred to as discontinuation (or withdrawal) symptoms, and they can include dizziness, feeling nauseous, unusual bodily sensations, anxiety and headaches. These symptoms are usually mild, but can sometimes be severe, especially if the antidepressant is stopped abruptly.
>
> If your antidepressant medication is being stopped, your GP should usually reduce the dose over a 4-week period.
>
> If you experience severe problems while reducing your medication, your GP might try you again on the original dose or try a similar antidepressant, and reduce again gradually while monitoring your symptoms.

Theses guidelines, first issued in 2004, marked a significant shift in official recognition of the difficulties people could have coming off SSRIs. In fact, it has emerged that withdrawal symptoms are associated with all antidepressants, including the older, but still frequently prescribed, tricyclics.

The guidance acknowledges a withdrawal syndrome but not other features of antidepressants that could qualify them as drugs of dependence. Tolerance can occur with SSRIs. One study (Fava, cited in Glenmullen 2001, p. 91) followed patients who had responded to treatment with 20mg of fluoxetine a day. After a year the drugs effect had worn off for 34 per cent of them. Most of the patients (83 per cent) responded to an increase to 40mg a day, but within a further year 27 per cent found it was no longer working.

Joseph Glenmullen (2005, p. 7) divides withdrawal symptoms into psychiatric and medical. He lists common psychiatric symptoms as depressed mood, low energy, crying uncontrollably, anxiety, insomnia, irritability, agitation, impulsivity, hallucinations, or suicidal or violent urges. It is no wonder that, in the absence of information to the contrary, people experiencing these symptoms have believed they cannot cope off their antidepressants. The dangerous suicidal or violent urges can occur any time there is a change in dose, up or down. He lists medical symptoms as including disabling dizziness, imbalance, nausea, vomiting, flu-like aches and pains, sweating, headaches, tremors, burning sensations, or electric shock-like 'zaps' in the brain. Altogether, he says, over 50 symptoms of antidepressant withdrawal have been identified. As with all drug effects, there is a great variation in the severity of symptoms people experience.

There is significant variation in the proportion of people who experience a withdrawal syndrome when stopping different SSRIs. Glenmullen cites a pair of studies showing a strong correlation between the half-life of the drug and the frequency of withdrawal reactions. Venlafaxine has a half-life of five hours and 78 per cent of people coming off it experienced a withdrawal reaction, whereas the corresponding figures for fluoxetine were four to six days and 14 per cent (Rosenbaum et al., Fava et al., cited in Glenmullen 2005, p. 84). However, Glenmullen believes the figure for fluoxetine to be an underestimate, as withdrawal reactions can take longer to emerge than was allowed for in the study. Table A2.3 in Appendix 2 shows the percentages of people in the *"All you need to know?"* survey (SAMH 2004) who experienced withdrawal reactions when coming off different SSRIs. These figures do not completely correlate with half-lives.

People coming off venlafaxine may start experiencing withdrawal symptoms within hours of stopping or missing a dose. For most SSRIs, they may appear two to five days after stopping, although for fluoxetine it may take up to 25 days for symptoms to appear (Glenmullen 2005, pp. 84–5).

NICE suggests a normal tapering period of four weeks and, in the guidance for professionals, says fluoxetine can usually be stopped in less time (NICE 2004b, p. 232). Glenmullen (2005, pp. 91–115) and Healy (2005 pp. 258–61) propose a withdrawal programme that may take considerably longer depending on the adverse effects of withdrawal the person encounters. Glenmullen (2005, p. 117) doesn't think tapering is usually necessary if the person has been on the drug for less than a month.

Although most people should be able to get off antidepressants successfully through tapering, Healy (2005, p. 257) writes: 'It has been clear for some time that treatment with SSRIs may set up a series of dyskinesias [involuntary movements] that persist for months or years after treatment halts. There are some grounds therefore to worry that treatment with SSRIs sets some people up for a perpetual cycle of neurological difficulties.'

NEUROLEPTICS

There is a strange silence about withdrawal from neuroleptics. A renowned manual for psychiatrists, *The Maudsley Prescribing Guidelines* (Taylor, Paton & Kerwin, 2007), has nothing to say about it at all, despite including material on withdrawal from other psychiatric drugs. NICE guidelines only say that it should be done slowly and the person should be monitored. There is no mention of possible adverse effects (NICE 2003, p. 67). Writing about neuroleptics, David Cohen (cited in Watkins 2006, p. 357) says, 'rational drug withdrawal may be the least studied topic in clinical psychopharmacology and the one about which clinicians are most ignorant'.

There may be several reasons for this silence. Along with antimanic medication, neuroleptics are the drugs mental health workers are most concerned with making sure people take. There is fear about what people might do if they stop taking them and who might be blamed. This emphasis occurs at all levels of the mental health system. It is enshrined in legislation, in protocols and job descriptions. Much of the time mental health workers spend with service users who are on these drugs is taken up with trying to ascertain if they are taking them properly. Depot injections are a way of ensuring that non-compliant patients are medicated at all times. With this mindset, it is not easy to also contemplate advising and supporting people to come off them.

Biomedical explanations for schizophrenia and bipolar disorder are more entrenched than for other diagnoses. The notion that drugs somehow compensate for chemical imbalances in the brain prevails. The implication of drugs for life has a strong hold on policy makers and practitioners even though there is evidence to suggest that, as a blanket policy, it isn't necessary and may do more harm than good.

The notion that once you are on neuroleptics you should stay on them is reinforced by alarming figures showing the rate of relapse when people stop taking them. For example, the *National Service Framework for Mental Health* (Department of Health 1999, p. 45), which set out how mental health services should be configured and delivered, included this statement about relapse: 'Some side effects of antipsychotic medication may lead people to discontinue their treatment. As relapse is five times as common if the service user does not take their prescribed medication non-compliance is likely to be a contributory factor in many cases of relapsing psychotic illness. It is therefore essential to adhere to prescribing guidelines.'

But figures such as these, showing high rates of relapse, come from questionable research methods and questionable interpretation of results. These are examined in 'A Critique of the Use of Neuroleptic Drugs' by David Cohen (1997, pp. 197–8). He points out that in these studies people have their medication stopped abruptly and then their rate of relapse is compared to that of people maintained on it. (In these studies what is considered to be relapse is variable and sometimes vague.) This method ignores the potential benefits of tapering, making it more likely that the people whose medication is stopped will relapse. In studies where medication was withdrawn gradually, the rate of relapse was very similar for those who had their medication withdrawn and those who stayed on it.

Examination of the data from these studies, including ones where medication was withdrawn abruptly, shows that people whose medication was stopped and who then relapsed tended to do so within three months. Commentators such as Baldessarini and Viguera (cited in Cohen 1997, p. 198) proposed that a psychotic episode so soon after ceasing to take medication is more likely to be withdrawal reaction than a relapse.

This interpretation of the data from withdrawal studies challenges the usual conclusion that people on neuroleptics can't come off them without a serious risk of relapse. Instead, it suggests that they show that some people can come off them safely, especially if they do so slowly. There is also an implication that, even if they do experience a psychotic episode after coming off their drugs, it may well be a one-off withdrawal symptom. If they can be helped through it, they may never experience another.

Research (Ballard et al. 2008) has demonstrated that it is possible for people with dementia to come off neuroleptics safely. Half of a group of 128 people diagnosed as having Alzheimer's disease (a form of dementia) had their drug replaced with a placebo. The neuroleptics were stopped in one go as these people were on low doses, as is usual when they are prescribed for people with dementia. After six months and a year there were no significant differences in functioning and symptoms between the two groups, except that the people who stayed on neuroleptics experienced a greater decline in verbal fluency. Yet, according to the researchers, people with dementia who are on neuroleptics are at increased risk of stroke, Parkinsonism, sedation, oedema (swelling caused by excess fluid in tissues), chest infections and death. Another paper (Ballard et al. 2009, pp. 151–7) revealed that three years after this research began 59 per cent of the people on placebo were still alive but only 30 per cent of those still on a neuroleptic.

People taking tranquillisers and antidepressants, and professionals who understood their struggles, were eventually able to establish evidence of withdrawal syndromes, despite opposition from drug companies and the medical establishment. So why hasn't this happened for neuroleptics?

The generally held belief that people should stay on them must be a major factor. But perhaps there are others. Tranquillisers and antidepressants have been taken by millions of people, many of whom have continued in roles such as parent, worker or student. It is a relatively ordinary experience. In contrast, people on neuroleptics are more likely to be seen as different, weird or mad, with mysterious conditions that can only be understood by specialist practitioners. They are more likely to be unemployed, socially marginalised and be attending mental health facilities. People taking any psychiatric drugs are liable to have their credibility challenged if they speak out, but perhaps this particularly applies to people on neuroleptics and antimanics.

There may be one more reason for the silence about withdrawing from neuroleptics. They can cause serious neurological problems – especially FGNs administered in high doses for long periods. But these may only emerge as doses are reduced. Perhaps sometimes it is just too uncomfortable for doctors to face the damage they can do.

But despite all this, there is a body of knowledge about withdrawal, and, in many respects it is similar to the knowledge about coming off other psychiatric drugs. Tapering is strongly recommended and Healy's three ways of distinguishing between withdrawal symptoms and new episodes of distress apply.

The following description of symptoms associated with withdrawal from neuroleptics is taken from John Watkins's book, *Healing Schizophrenia* (2006, p. 363). He lists common physical symptoms that can accompany rapid withdrawal as anxiety, insomnia, restlessness, and flu-like symptoms such as headache, nausea, aches and pains, malaise, sweating, runny nose, diarrhoea and vomiting.

He also draws attention to extrapyramidal symptoms (stiffness, shaking, restlessness and involuntary movements) which may emerge for the first time or get worse with neuroleptic dose reduction. Most will disappear, though it may take several months for them to do so. One of them, tardive dyskinesia, may not disappear at all.

Watkins draws on the work of Chouinard and Jones (cited in Watkins 2006, p. 365) to describe the specific characteristics of psychosis that can occur during withdrawal. Specific features are:

- psychotic symptoms appear soon – usually within days or weeks of either stopping neuroleptic medication or substantially reducing the dosage;
- the psychosis involves positive symptoms (e.g. suspiciousness, hallucinations, delusions) but not negative symptoms (emotional withdrawal, blunted effect);
- the psychosis may be even more severe than it was before treatment and might involve the emergence of some new, previously unreported symptom;
- signs of growing treatment resistance may have been present prior to stopping medication (i.e. gradually increasing dosages required to control the symptoms);
- symptoms of tardive dyskinesia are often present and may be severe;
- signs of neuroleptic-induced sexual dysfunction, such as reduced sexual drive, are often present.

This list may be sufficiently alarming to put both patients and practitioners off withdrawal. But it should be noted that even when people are taken off neuroleptics abruptly nearly half do not experience psychosis as a withdrawal symptom or relapse. But it does provide a reason to come off slowly and carefully. There isn't a formula for how slowly. The method most recommended is to reduce in small steps and stay at each stage long enough for any symptoms to emerge and subside before moving on to the next one. Depot injections, because they are slow-release, have their own inbuilt taper, but people coming off them will still be taking less of a risk if they do so in stages.

Watkins (2006, p. 366–7) also writes usefully about the psychological changes people may experience when coming off psychiatric drugs, and although his focus is coming off neuroleptics, what he has to say could also apply to other drugs:

> An important result of reducing or stopping medication – one that is often overlooked – concerns the changes which may subsequently occur in a diagnosed person's emotional state, motivation and general level of vitality. If the original medication had a suppressing or dampening effect, reducing the dose may result in a substantial release of physical and mental energy, together with an unmasking of previously attenuated feelings. While this is generally a positive and welcome development, removal of the stress buffer which neuroleptic drugs provide could leave some extremely sensitive individuals feeling exposed and vulnerable.

Much of what Watkins and others have to say about coming off neuroleptics is about preparing for life without them.

People on neuroleptics may also be taking anti-Parkinson's drugs to alleviate extrapyramidal effects. They too are associated with withdrawal symptoms. Peter Breggin and David Cohen (1999, p. 168) list flu-like symptoms such as nausea, vomiting, chills, weakness, and headaches, as well as insomnia and restlessness. As always, these can be minimised by withdrawing slowly.

One final point about neuroleptics –both tolerance and withdrawal symptoms are associated with taking them. NICE guidelines (2003, p. 59) acknowledge tolerance rather obscurely by referring to people taking neuroleptics for the first time as 'drug-naïve': 'Evidence suggests that drug-naïve patients may respond to relatively lower doses of antipsychotic drugs.'

ANTIMANICS

There has been even less research into the effects of coming off lithium than there has been into coming off neuroleptics. But the issues are similar. The diagnosis of bipolar disorder is generally seen as a diagnosis for life and the emphasis is on compliance rather than coming off. David Cohen (1997, p. 198) reports that studies of people stopping lithium treatment reflect those of people stopping neuroleptics. If lithium is stopped abruptly they are frequently seen to relapse by having a manic episode, but tapered withdrawal is associated with fewer such episodes. The speed with which they occur suggests that they are in fact withdrawal symptoms rather than 'new illness episodes'.

David Healy (2005, p. 100) suggests that up to half of people coming off lithium will have a withdrawal problem – one that can be minimised by coming off slowly. Apart from mania, other withdrawal symptoms can include anxiety, irritability, tension, restlessness and sleep disturbance. Like people coming off other drugs that damp down feelings, people coming off lithium may find they feel more alert, emotional and energetic than before. This may be exactly what they hope for, but can initially be alarming and take some getting used to.

Most knowledge about coming off anticonvulsants, such as carbamazepine and valproate, comes from the experience of people prescribed them to control epilepsy. There is a familiar litany of symptoms associated with withdrawal and some novel ones. The following lists are taken from Mind's pamphlet, *Making Sense of Coming Off Psychiatric Drugs* (Darton 2005, pp. 20–1). For carbamazepine they include aching muscles, spasms or twitches, walking unsteadily, sleeping problems, no energy or appetite, headaches, tension, weak memory and loss of concentration. It can also make people feel depressed and irritable. There are reports of some people developing low blood pressure with a fast heartbeat. For valproate, they include anxiety and restlessness, muscle twitching, tremors, weakness, nausea and vomiting. There is a small risk of having a seizure, even for people who haven't had one before. Once again, these symptoms can be minimised by coming off slowly.

SUMMARY

To sum up the evidence of withdrawal from psychiatric drugs, every drug is associated with withdrawal symptoms but approximately half of those coming off their drugs do not experience them, even if they come off abruptly. For others, the effects can be minimised by reducing their dosage gradually, i.e. tapering. But there may be a small proportion of people who have great difficulties coming off, however slowly.

Life after Coming off Psychiatric Drugs

We have already seen that the majority of people prescribed tranquillisers and antidepressants are expected to stop taking them at some point. Given the right information and support, nearly all can be expected to succeed in stopping. There is far less agreement that people on neuroleptics and antimanic drugs should stop taking them, though plenty try, and some succeed. But once people have got through the process of withdrawal, what happens? How many are back on their medication a year later or five years later?

The answer to this question is crucial. How can good advice about coming off or staying on drugs be given without this information? And there are other questions. Given that some people succeed in staying off and others don't, what makes the difference? Take two people with diagnoses of schizophrenia. Is there anything about them that means it could be predicted that one is more likely to succeed in staying off their drugs than the other? It could be their age, the duration of their distress or the form it takes, their social situation, motivation to be off medication, employment prospects, self-esteem – a host of factors. And is there anything mental health professionals can do to help them to improve their chances of staying off? Should they stay in contact with mental health services or cut their ties? Does defining their experiences in ways other than the medical model help? Can therapy make a difference?

Basically, we don't know. There is a glaring gap in our knowledge about what eventually happens to people who come off medication. For people on neuroleptics or antimanics, this matters a great deal. If it can be shown that significant numbers of people are getting off these drugs and staying off successfully, others will feel encouraged to try. But if there is irrefutable evidence that those who succeed in getting through the withdrawal stage invariably end up back on them a year or so later, people will be more willing to consider staying on them. Which of these is true is of great consequence, which is why a paper 'Factors Involved in Outcome and Recovery in Schizophrenia Patients Not on Antipsychotic Medications: A 15-Year Multifollow-Up Study' (Harrow & Jobe 2007, pp. 406–14) is so significant.

The study aimed to address two questions: can people come off and stay off neuroleptics successfully and, if so, are there are ways of predicting who stands the best chance of success? It did so by studying over a period of 15 years the progress of 145 patients who were admitted to psychiatric hospitals in Chicago and put on neuroleptics. Of these, 64 were diagnosed with schizophrenia; the others had various other diagnoses including bipolar disorder and depression. At the beginning of the study they were all assessed for various characteristics that could affect their success in recovery. These included 'early developmental achievements' based on such matters as work history, education, marital status and IQ; and the nature of their 'illness', such as whether the onset was acute and if it included depressive symptoms. Recovery was defined as the absence of psychosis and negative symptoms, and adequate psychosocial functioning. Various scales were used to measure degree of recovery.

After 15 years, 31 per cent of the people diagnosed with schizophrenia were not on any psychiatric drugs, 61 per cent were still on neuroleptics (with or without other medication) and a further 8 per cent were on other medication. The researchers found that people not taking any psychiatric drugs tended to function better than those still on neuroleptics. For example, 64 per cent of people on neuroleptics were experiencing psychotic activity but only 28 per cent of people who had stopped their medication were. Also, 19 of the 23 people with the poorest outcomes were still on neuroleptics.

Of those diagnosed with schizophrenia, 12 (19 per cent) were deemed to be in recovery. They were 40 per cent of the people not on any psychiatric drugs (8 out of 20), 5 per cent of people on neuroleptics (2 out of 39) and 40 per cent of people on psychiatric drugs other than neuroleptics (2 out of 5). There were similar results for the people with diagnoses other than schizophrenia, with those who were no longer on neuroleptics again faring significantly better.

These results leave us with a question. Did the people who were not on neuroleptics do better because they had come off their drugs, or were they people who might have been expected to do better anyway, in which case no longer being on neuroleptics could be seen as an outcome of doing better rather than a cause? The researchers looked at the factors which may have determined outcomes and concluded, 'The results suggest that the subgroup of schizophrenia patients not on medications was different in terms of being a self-selected group having better early prognosis and developmental potential.'

In other words, they could have been predicted to be more likely to recover. But this is only part of the story. There were people with similarly good prospects of recovery based on 'better early prognosis and developmental potential' who stayed on neuroleptics and were not as successful in recovery as those who stopped taking them. But the people who came off their drugs tended to have a stronger sense of being in control of their lives and greater self-esteem than those who stayed on. Whether these characteristics caused people to stop taking their drugs or resulted from not taking their drugs (or a combination of both) isn't clear. The research didn't look at the circumstances in which decisions about taking or not taking drugs were made.

Harrow and Job point out that people who stop taking their drugs successfully and leave mental health services do not come to the attention of mental health workers, whereas people who relapse are likely to end up back in the system. This tends to reinforce a view that all people diagnosed with schizophrenia need to stay on their drugs for life, a view that is challenged by this research.

The research did not seek to challenge the medical model of diagnosis and routine use of neuroleptics. It did not look at people's attempts to come off medication and whether following good practice principles, such as coming off very slowly, resulted in better outcomes. But it does show people diagnosed with schizophrenia doing well, over long periods of time, without taking neuroleptics. This is significant. It also suggests factors which can aid success. The downside is the implication that certain characteristics predict an inability to live successfully without neuroleptics. But characteristics are not necessarily fixed. If, for example, self-esteem makes a difference, then perhaps more attention should be put on helping people to build their self-esteem.

This study is unusual. The *BMJ* editorial, also quoted from in Chapter 1 (Turner 2004, p. 1059), concluded: 'An outstanding need remains for...long-term studies of outcome and treatments over decades rather than a few months. Such research fits poorly with the short-term pressures of the research assessment exercise, drug company marketing policies or career advancement.'

There is the same need for such long-term research about all diagnoses and treatments. People's views about their own experiences can and should make a major contribution to it. Until the evidence of the long-term effectiveness of staying on or coming off drugs is firmly established, factors other than evidence will hold sway. The tendency has been for a 'one size fits all' approach to predominate, based on a crude diagnosis/chemical imbalance/drugs for life approach. The next three chapters include evidence from people who have successfully come off their psychiatric drugs which offers some challenge to that approach.

Critical Reflection Box 3.1

Reducing or Giving up a Drug

This exercise is intended to help you reflect on what it is like to try to reduce or come off a drug.

What are the similarities and differences between trying to reduce or come off psychiatric drugs and social drugs such as alcohol, caffeine and nicotine?

What are the similarities and differences between trying to reduce or come off psychiatric drugs and street drugs (illegal drugs)?

If you have tried to reduce or come off a psychiatric, social or street drug answer the questions below. If you haven't, you could try talking to someone who has and asking for their responses to the questions.

1. What was your motivation?
2. Did you ask for or receive any support? How was that?
3. How did you go about it, e.g. did you stop abruptly or reduce gradually? How was that?
4. Did you experience any adverse effects as you withdrew from the drug? If so, what were they?
5. If you succeeded, (a) did you have any setbacks or difficulties after you first reduced or stopped taking the drug, and (b) what have been the benefits?
6. If you didn't succeed, (a) what was that like, and (b) did you learn anything from the experience?

4
Coping with Coming Off: Making the Decision

Doing Our Own Research

The mental health charity, Mind, has taken an interest in people's experiences of trying to come off psychiatric drugs since its involvement in the *That's Life! Survey on tranquillisers* (Lacey & Woodward 1985). This survey exposed how commonly people had great difficulty in stopping taking tranquillisers. A report published in 2001, *Mind's Yellow Card for Reporting Drug Side Effects* (Cobb, Darton & Juttla 2001), included a section which highlighted the range of experiences associated with withdrawal from all psychiatric drugs (p. 23): 'Outcomes varied enormously from emphatically good outcomes – 'back in the real world, not a zombie' – to getting ill again or 'back to square one'.

It was to find out why this variation occurred and what could be done to improve people's experiences of coming off drugs that Mind decided to commission an in-depth survey. Funding was obtained from the Department of Health for a survey which would comprise about 200 short interviews with people who had tried coming off psychiatric drugs, with 50 follow-up depth interviews.

There was one notable change from the *That's Life!* survey. The authors of that report made much of the input of medical experts (p. 20): 'We consulted with numerous doctors, specialists and psychiatrists over the sorts of questions and general shape of the survey.'

But there was no mention of people who had taken tranquillisers being consulted. By 2003 it was inconceivable that the experience and expertise of people who had tried coming off psychiatric drugs themselves would not be used to contribute to the survey. But Mind went several steps further. It decided to offer the contract to a group of people with this experience who, between them, had the necessary research skills to carry out the work.

The Coping with Coming Off (CWCO) survey became, then, a piece of user-led research which shaped it in several significant ways. Most obviously, it blurred the distinction between the researcher and the researched. The research team also became the first participants in the survey, interviewing each other. And all the people we interviewed were treated as participants in the research rather than subjects. We asked them not just to describe their experiences, but to reflect and comment on them. Some of the information they shared was personal and could be distressing. Undoubtedly the promise of confidentiality was essential in making this possible. Knowing they were talking to people who had tried coming off psychiatric drugs themselves may also have made it easier to feel safe and talk openly and honestly.

Although most of the work on the CWCO project was done by people with direct experience of trying to come off psychiatric drugs, there was also a great deal of valuable input from others. The research team was backed up by Mind's policy department throughout. An advisory group was made up of people with a variety of expertise and included a psychiatrist and a pharmacist. Initial findings from the short interviews were presented to workshops at Mind's annual conference and participants were asked to suggest lines of inquiry for the depth interviews. The findings from all of the research were shared at a stakeholder conference and the people present were asked to make suggestions for the action and recommendations section of the report. This conference was addressed by Mike Shooter, who had recently retired as President of the Royal College of Psychiatrists and who had publicly spoken of his own experience of being on antidepressants. The research was 'user-led' but also a collaboration which included the Department of Health as the funding agency.

RECRUITING PARTICIPANTS

Participants were recruited through networks of service users/survivors. They volunteered themselves. Recruiting people this way is very different from the more usual method of seeking the approval of ethics committees to contact people though the services they use. They were recruited as citizens rather than patients.

We intended to recruit significantly more volunteers willing to participate in the research than we actually needed. Then we could select from them a balanced group in terms of success or not in coming off, experience of different psychiatric drugs, and characteristics in terms of age, gender, ethnicity and place of residence. Because of the nature of the grant, we were restricted to people living in England and, because of Mind's focus on the mental health of adults, we decided not to include anyone under the age of 18. Mind's previous experience of surveys suggested it would be fairly easy to find enough people from which to choose our sample. For instance, for *Mind's Yellow Card for Reporting Drug Side Effects* (Cobb, Darton & Juttla 2001), 502 people wrote in to report their experiences of adverse effects of psychiatric drugs.

Potential participants were asked to complete and return a brief form which gave us enough information for us to be able to select a suitable sample. The form was distributed through Mind's networks and was available on its website. We also used e-groups and personal contacts, and other organisations helped out by copying and distributing the form. But completed forms did not arrive in the numbers we hoped for. We are not sure why it was difficult to recruit enough people, but there were some clues in comments we received. One person confided:

> *I think what you're doing is really important, but I can't talk about my experience. It was too painful.*

Someone who did volunteer to take part, who had a difficult time coming off a tranquilliser, still told us:

> *I'm so bored with the whole thing; I just want to get on with my life. I'm not talking about your interview, but generally I've had a gut full of it.*

In the end we were able to obtain 248 completed forms. Fortunately, from these we were able to select enough people to interview and still have a balance in key areas. We carried out 204 short interviews. Table 4.1 shows how successful participants were in coming off their drugs. Our priority was for about half the people we interviewed to have completely succeeded in coming off the drug(s), and this we were able to achieve.

Table 4.1 How successful people were in coming off the drug(s) (%)*

Completely successful	48
Partially successful	21
Not successful	23
Still ongoing, not sure yet	8

* Percentages have been rounded up or down to the nearest whole number and don't always add up to exactly 100 per cent.

As with nearly every other question we asked, the question about success was not always straightforward to answer, illustrating the complexity of the experience of being on and coming off psychiatric drugs. For example, one person said they had been completely successful in coming off a drug but it didn't feel like a success because they were struggling emotionally. Another had succeeded in stopping their drug but six months later had to go back on another. But they rated their experience a success because they preferred the drug they went on to the one they came off. We could have come up with an objective measure of success, but felt the benefits of that approach were outweighed by our belief in the importance of people making their own personal judgements.

In both the short and depth interviews we focused on one episode of trying to come off a drug or drugs. Usually it was the most recent, but we gave participants the opportunity to talk about an episode that was more significant to them, if they wished.

Table 4.2 shows the types of drugs people had taken. Many had taken more than one.

We wanted to see how people's experiences varied according to which type of psychiatric drugs they were coming off. We also looked at factors such as how long people had been on the drug they came off and how fast they came off it. To find answers to these particular questions we had to exclude the 73 people who tried coming off more than one drug in the episode they told us about. Table 4.3 shows what types of drugs the remaining 131 people had tried coming off.

Because of the low number of people coming off tranquillisers, we did not include them in our calculations. The antidepressant venlafaxine (Efexor) was included with SSRIs. Although classified as a serotonin noradrenaline reuptake inhibitor (SNRI), it is closely related to SSRIs. The numbers of people coming off neuroleptics and antimanics were quite low, and so when making comparisons about coming off different types of drugs, we have avoided drawing conclusions from small percentage differences.

Table 4.2 The drug(s) people had taken (%)

Tranquillisers	40
Antidepressants	75
Neuroleptics	46
Antimanics	29
Other	13

Table 4.3 People coming off a single drug (no.)*

Tranquillisers	11
SSRIs	67
Neuroleptics	33
Antimanics	20
Total	*131*

*The figures include people who tried to come off a single drug while staying on one or more others. They differ from the figures in the report *Coping with Coming Off* (Read 2005), where we only considered people coming off a single drug who were not on any other drug.

We wanted to make sure we included sufficient people from BME communities to be able to see if their experiences differed from those of the majority population. We aimed for 20 per cent and ended up with 19 per cent, or 38 people. We included in this category people from Africa, Asia, the Caribbean, Eastern Europe and Ireland, and people with heritage from these places, including people who described themselves as mixed race. We also included people who identified as Jewish, Romany and Semitic.

No one group predominated, so we had to consider the BME group as a whole. Different BME communities do not have the same relationships with mental health services and so it was not obvious that differences between this group and the non-BME participants would be evident. It turned out that they were. This began with the profile of what drugs they were on when they tried coming off one or more. Of the BME group 70 per cent were on a neuroleptic or antimanic compared with only 45 percent of the other participants.

Our biggest challenge in choosing a balanced group to interview was in finding enough men, and we ended up with only 36 per cent of participants being male. However, gender, age and where people lived (rural or urban) did not turn out to be significant in determining their experience of trying to come off drugs.

It was easier to achieve a balanced sample for the depth interviews as we were choosing 50 people from 204. We completed 46 interviews. A statistical breakdown of the sample has not been included here because the information we were collecting was basically qualitative in nature.

METHODS, STRENGTHS AND LIMITATIONS

The short interviews were intended to provide statistical information and a questionnaire was devised. Participants were interviewed by telephone unless it was more convenient to meet. The length of the interviews averaged about 25 minutes. It was challenging to relate what were sometimes complex and personal experiences to a questionnaire of tick boxes and scales, but worth it. Significant statistical information was generated and these interviews helped us to identify topics for inclusion in the depth interviews. The completed questionnaires tended to be covered with additional notes and observations, some of which provided material for this account of the research. Data analysis was carried out using a computer program called KeyPoint. The short interviews were conducted during 2003–4.

The depth interviews were semi-structured and intended to illuminate issues identified from the short interviews. They averaged 45 minutes and were conducted on the telephone or in person, recorded and transcribed. They were carried out in 2004. Our analysis was based on a method called 'Framework', which was developed at the National Centre for Social Research. Interviews were scrutinised and a list of topics identified. Each interview was then coded according to topic. This enabled us to follow a topic across all the interviews and it was then possible to see themes emerging. In this way, we were able to analyse large amounts of qualitative information and produce a more sophisticated and nuanced account of the research findings than if we had been restricted to the quantitative analysis. The depth interviews have also served as a source of illustrative quotations. (Some of these have been lightly edited for clarity and brevity, but care has been taken to avoid changing the meaning of them in any way.)

Recruiting participants in the research through networks of service users/survivors will inevitably have introduced an element of bias into the research. We can say with some certainty that the people interviewed were not completely typical of all people who have tried to stop taking their drugs, but can only speculate about possible differences. They may, for example, have been better informed and had more sense of being entitled to act on their own initiative than the average person taking psychiatric drugs. It is possible that people with more 'interesting stories' had a greater incentive to volunteer to be interviewed. Certainly one person we spoke to had ruled herself out because she felt her experience was insignificant. She had only taken one tablet of an antidepressant before deciding to stop because of an extreme reaction to it. She was persuaded to take part. We were relying on people's memories and their knowledge of what they had been taking. We didn't ask about dosages because we didn't expect enough people would have known or remembered the dosages of the drugs they were taking, and so we were unable to see how that factor influenced people's experience of trying to come off their drugs.

We think that the strength of the research is that we succeeded in capturing people's stories; the emerging themes and instructive anecdotes, as well as the statistics. People shared their thoughts and feelings, mistakes and triumphs, and sometimes their secrets. We were able to build up a detailed picture of how decisions were made, of negotiations with doctors, how information was or wasn't obtained and what people learned from their experiences, whether or not they regarded them as successful. We believe that the research identified some key and unresolved issues regarding power and control between doctors and their patients – who is ultimately in charge of decisions about taking or stopping psychiatric drugs.

We captured the struggles of people coming off SSRIs to make sense of the feelings and sensations they experienced and have them acknowledged by their doctors. We saw how many people, especially those taking neuroleptics, decided they were better off not telling their doctors they had decided to stop taking their drugs. And we learned how successful people were in stopping and staying off their drugs when they had taken this autonomous action (or been non-compliant, depending on your point of view). We also came across enough examples of good communication and understanding between patients and doctors to feel encouraged that conflict isn't inherent, difficult situations can be negotiated and the relationship can be a genuine partnership.

This account of the research follows the three stages of trying to come off psychiatric drugs identified in Chapter 3. First there is the decision to come off – the events and thoughts that lead up to it and how the decision is made. Then there is the period of reducing or stopping the drug – how the person goes about it and what they experience. Finally, it becomes apparent what the outcome is – complete success or something else. With this, lessons may be learned as people look back and reflect on their actions.

The Decision to Try Coming off Psychiatric Drugs

To understand people's motivations for wanting to come off their drugs, we needed to know how they viewed their experience of being

Table 4.4 How well or badly drugs have worked for people overall (%)

	All	SSRIs	Neuroleptics	Antimanics	BME	Non-BME
Mainly helpful	18	24	6	15	18	17
Some helpful, some made no difference	7	7	9	15	3	8
Some helpful, some harmful	32	42	30	35	30	33
Mainly made no difference	4	4	3	0	3	5
Mainly harmful	21	9	24	25	37	17
Other	18	13	27	10	11	19

on them. We decided to ask them to evaluate their entire experience on psychiatric drugs, not just the one(s) they decided to try to come off. This was to give a sense of their overall attitude to them.

Table 4.4 shows that 18 per cent found drugs to be mainly helpful, with a similar proportion (21 per cent) saying they were mainly harmful. The highest figure, 32 per cent, was for the category 'some helpful, some harmful', which illustrates the complexity of people's experiences. This is reinforced by the 18 per cent who didn't find any of the five choices on offer appropriate and opted for 'other'.

An example of the complexity of some people's experience was provided by a participant who shared three instances of being on different drugs. Already on an antidepressant and tranquilliser, she was prescribed lithium:

> *It was awful. The shakes were terrible; I couldn't walk properly or see properly.*

She came off the lithium when her daughter visited and said, 'You're not taking these, Mum, they're toxic', and threw them in the bin. On another occasion she was admitted to hospital and put on sertraline (Lustral), an SSRI:

> *They* [the tablets] *did not suit me at all. I was dry-retching all the time. They kept saying, 'when they kick in you'll be all right', but they never did kick in.*

Eventually, after seven weeks, her consultant was persuaded to take her off sertraline, and she was put on mirtazapine (Zispin), a noradrenergic and specific serotonergic antidepressant:

> *It worked almost immediately, in about three days. I wasn't better, but I knew I was going to get better. I remember waking up on 29 September and knowing I was going to get better. I always say it was my second birthday.*

Other people had mixed experiences of one drug. One person told us about a tranquilliser:

> *Diazepam saved my life, but I can't get off it.*

A number of people in the survey were in favour of psychiatric drugs as a short-term emergency measure but not for long-term use. One man was taking a neuroleptic, an antimanic and an antidepressant. He told us:

> *If I'm going to have a crisis, I don't think the medication I'm on makes a lot of difference.*

But:

> *I think taking quite high doses of medication for a short period helps me get through a crisis.*

The columns headed 'SSRIs', 'neuroleptics' and 'antimanics' show how people who decided to try coming off these drugs rated all of the drugs they had taken. It shows that people coming off SSRIs had a more positive experience of psychiatric drugs overall than people coming off neuroleptics. Nearly a quarter of people coming off SSRIs (24 per cent) said drugs had been mainly helpful, nearly twice as many as those who said they were mainly harmful (13 per cent). In contrast, only 6 per cent of people coming off neuroleptics said they had found drugs mainly helpful and four times as many (24 per cent) said they were mainly harmful. More people trying to come off antimanics rated their drugs as mainly harmful (25 per cent) than mainly helpful (15 per cent).

There is a contrast between people from BME communities and others. Although the figures for 'mainly helpful' were similar, people from BME communities were more than twice as likely to rate drugs as mainly harmful (37 per cent compared with 17 per cent). Some, but not all, of this difference can be accounted for by the people from

BME communities being more likely to have taken neuroleptics and antimanics.

We also thought it important to know how much choice people had over taking their drugs. As can be seen from Table 4.5, we gave them the opportunity to choose from several options between compulsion and free choice.

Table 4.5 shows that 30 per cent of participants had been legally compelled to take psychiatric drugs at some point. The highest figures for all the participants, considered together, were 70 per cent for feeling pressured to take them, or powerless or passive about taking them. The biggest contrast was between people trying to come off an SSRI and people trying to come off a neuroleptic or antimanic. Only 3 per cent of the SSRI people had been compelled to take medication compared with 58 per cent of people coming off a neuroleptic and 55 per cent of those coming off an antimanic. People from BME communities were more likely to have been compelled to take medication than the other (non-BME) participants (47 per cent compared with 27 per cent).

Overall, Tables 4.4 and 4.5 show that many of the participants had bad experiences of psychiatric drugs and had not positively signed up to being on them. People coming off neuroleptics and people from BME communities were particularly likely to have had this combination of

Table 4.5 The degree of choice in taking psychiatric drug(s) (%)*

	All	SSRIs	Neuroleptics	Antimanics	BME	Non-BME
Been compelled to take them under Mental Health Act	30	3	58	55	47	27
Felt that if did not comply, would be compelled	52	27	84	80	71	50
Felt pressurised to take them	70	62	78	89	73	72
Felt powerless or passive about taking them	70	61	81	90	74	71
Felt had a free choice about taking them	54	78	47	70	49	60
Other experiences about choice	22	21	24	10	16	23

*Participants were able to give more than one answer.

experiences. For some people, deciding to come off the drugs was about restoring a sense of being in control of their own lives.

> *I made a decision and carried it through and did something for myself. Rather than being in a sick role, where you're a sort of helpless patient, I became a bit more of an active agent. I moved from that passive role to an active one where I was back in control. I got back a bit of my life and that knocked on to other things. I had a little more about me. I was pleased I had actually done that. It changed my identity a bit – some-body who wasn't sort of reliant on medication or just doing what the doctor said.*

Having acquired this background information we were ready to ask people about one episode of trying to come off their drugs. We began by asking why they had tried to do it.

Table 4.6 shows that the most common reason for all participants was not liking the adverse effects, given by 60 per cent. The discussion of adverse effects in Chapter 2 shows that they are not just 'unpleasant' but can be life-threatening or life-destroying. But people

Table 4.6   The reasons for wanting to come off drug(s) (%)*

	All	SSRIs	Neuroleptics	Antimanics	BME	Non-BME
I didn't like the adverse effects of the drugs	60	54	76	70	71	58
I didn't like the idea of being on them long term	53	57	52	55	58	52
I felt better or things were better in my life and I didn't need them	37	45	24	45	39	36
The drugs were not useful	32	33	24	50	34	32
I had only expected to be on them for a limited time	19	19	18	21	5	18
I was advised to come off them by the doctor	7	3	6	10	3	8
Other	34	22	36	40	39	33

*People could give more than one reason.

may be prepared to put up with a great deal if the drugs are effective in controlling symptoms. Often it is difficult to weigh up the benefits and disadvantages of a drug. How do you balance possible long-term damage to health against immediate benefits in symptom reduction? Doctors, friends and family members may see things differently from the person taking the drug, valuing evident changes in behaviour and being less concerned with the impact of adverse effects. A decision to stop taking a drug because of adverse effects may not be supported by mental health professionals and be seen as an act of non-compliance.

The second most common reason for wanting to come off drugs was not liking the idea of being on them long term, given by 53 per cent. Within this desire, there were several strands of thought. For some people, it was fear of the damage the drugs could do if they were taken for a long time. In some instances this fear was about specific health threats known to be associated with particular drugs; in others it was a more general concern about putting chemicals into their bodies year after year:

> *I wouldn't say my attitude to all medication is very negative, but I find it hard to conceptualise that I should be given something that should heal me in one aspect but would be destroying and poisoning my body in another aspect.*

Another set of ideas was about wanting to be 'your true self'. This could be about feelings, thoughts or perceptions. Again, it could be difficult to persuade others, such as doctors, and family, that this was the right course to follow, especially as you might be 'doing well' on the medication in terms of the balance between symptom relief and obvious adverse effects. A decision to come off for these reasons could be construed positively (independence, empowerment, recovery) or not (non-compliance):

> *I felt a bit controlled by this drug in that when I thought something I didn't know if it was me thinking it or the drug making me think it.*

For another participant, staying on lithium meant:

> *I would be swallowing this tablet every single day forever and I would never really know my own emotions truly again.*

A participant who came off a tranquilliser explained how being on this drug undermined her confidence:

Say I managed to go abroad again and I lost my pills, I would be vulnerable to something external. It wasn't like I had internal strengths. My sanity and existence were dependent on whether or not I had the pills with me which gradually, gradually made me feel more rather than less vulnerable. Every time I took a pill I was concerned. It made me feel that if I hadn't taken a pill I would have gone crazy. So that was increasing my anxiety rather than lowering it.

The third most common reason for wanting to come off drugs was 'I felt better or things were better in my life and I didn't need them.' Although not always the case, this could be because the drugs were seen to have done their job of assisting someone through a difficult time. It is notable that people coming off an SSRI or antimanic (both 45 per cent) were more likely to give this as a reason than people coming off a neuroleptic (24 per cent).

Among the 34 per cent who said 'other', the most common reason was never having wanted to be on the drugs in the first place. Other reasons given included: swapping to another drug; wanting to avoid the stigma of being on drugs; wanting to see if they could manage without; and wanting to get pregnant without the risk of being on psychiatric drugs.

Generally, figures for people coming off specific types of drugs were broadly similar. But people trying to come off neuroleptics (76 per cent) and antimanics (70 per cent) were more likely to have done so because of adverse effects than people on SSRIs (54 per cent). Half (50 per cent) of people on an antimanic said it wasn't useful; a higher figure than for SSRIs (33 per cent) and neuroleptics (24 per cent). There were no great differences between the figures for people from BME communities and other participants.

In the literature about people stopping their psychiatric drugs there is often an emphasis on irrational motives for doing so. Motives are always open to interpretation, but this survey indicates that people's motives are often rational and well thought through. Some people did, however, 'own up' to having tried coming off for not the best of reasons, as the following three examples illustrate:

This counsellor told me that I'd started to go through a teenage rebellion period when I was in my late 30s. And I think some of this non-compliance

Critical Reflection Box 4.1

Deciding Whether to Come off Psychiatric Drugs

'Tips for coming off psychiatric medication' is an extract from an article 'Coming off medication?' written by Guy Holmes and Marese Hudson, which gives advice to people who are thinking about coming off their psychiatric drugs. You will find further details about the article in Appendix 1.

1. Draw two sets of the four boxes shown below with the headings but not the other content.
2. Think of two people you know well who are on psychiatric drugs.
3. Read the instructions on using the boxes.
4. Fill in one set of boxes for each person you have thought of, doing your best to put yourself in their shoes.
5. Decide if you would try coming off your medication if you were in their shoes.

Tips for coming off psychiatric medication

Be sure that you want to try and come off your medication. Think through the pros and cons of coming off and staying on your drugs. One of the best ways to do this is to 'brainstorm' four lists (see below). Only write down things that you feel are important to you (not what you 'ought' to put down). Once the lists are complete, you may be more aware of the mixed feelings you have about being on drugs and be in a position to make a judgement about whether, overall, you want to stay on or come off your drugs. Do the advantages of coming off medication outweigh the disadvantages? Where does the balance lie? The lists may also identify areas you can start to tackle before starting the withdrawal process.

Making the decision to stop or carry on taking medication

Pros of coming off	*Cons of coming off*
e.g. 'I won't feel zombied out' 'I'll feel more confident if my weight returns to normal' 'I can drive' 'It will confirm I'm better'	e.g. 'I might have another breakdown' 'My husband might get uptight/get on at me'

Pros of staying on	*Cons of staying on*
e.g. 'I don't risk the withdrawal effects' 'I'm quite stable'	e.g. 'Side effects: lethargy, weight gain' 'Sex life is affected' 'I don't like doing what others think is best for me'

I've had with my medication was due to feeling rebellious. I came to the conclusion that was part of it because – apart from the fact that I felt I didn't always need to take this drug cocktail they were giving me – I think some of the need to stop taking them was just my way of getting back at the medical profession.

If I'm really honest, I think I usually make these decisions at the wrong time. It was during the summer when I wasn't seeing a therapist, and that is usually the kind of thing I do. I think that's part of the problem really, that I have this rather self-destructive thread running through.

I was high and didn't think I needed them.

Next, we wanted to know about how people's doctors were or were not involved in decisions about trying to come off. In Table 4.7, we start with the least levels of involvement of doctors – coming off against a doctor's advice or without telling them – through more collaborative decision making to the doctor making the decision.

The figure that stands out is the 47 per cent of people from BME communities who decided to try to come off their drug(s) without telling their doctor – more than twice the figure of 22 per cent for the other participants. In nearly all instances, the first two categories can be seen as the person being non-compliant. There was only one exception from

Table 4.7 How the decision to try to come off was made (%)

	All	SSRIs	Neuroleptics	Antimanics	BME	Non-BME
I decided against the advice of my doctor	12	10	15	20	18	11
I decided without telling my doctor	26	18	36	25	47	22
I decided and my doctor accepted this	28	39	21	30	21	30
It was a joint decision between me and my doctor	13	18	9	15	5	15
My doctor decided and I accepted this	9	9	12	0	5	10
Other	11	6	6	10	3	12

Table 4.8   The degree of non-compliance (%)

All	39
SSRIs	28
Neuroleptics	52
Antimanics	45
BME	66
Non-BME	33

the depth interviews:

> *I haven't told my GP but we've kind of had an understanding over the years. He pretty much allows me to self-medicate. I know he would have said 'Yes, that's fine.'*

Table 4.8 combines the first two categories to show the degree of non-compliance among the different groups.

People from BME communities stand out as being the least compliant group: 66 per cent compared with 33 per cent of other participants. Their more antagonistic relationship with medication and doctors compared with the other participants can be traced back through the previous tables. They were more likely to rate their experience of drugs as mainly harmful and more likely to have been compelled to take them or feared being compelled to take them.

Similarly, people who were trying to come off neuroleptics or antimanics were more non-compliant than people trying to come off SSRIs and had a more antagonistic relationship with psychiatric drugs. They were more likely to rate them as mainly harmful and more likely to have been compelled or feared being compelled to take them.

Neuroleptics and antimanics are more likely to be seen as drugs for life than SSRIs. Mental health workers are often preoccupied with making sure they are being taken. So stopping them is more likely to be seen as an act of defiance than stopping SSRIs.

> *There's this fear of being forced into compliance. I know I'm being a bit covert and underhand but the threat has been offered.*

This survey shows up clear distinctions between the overall experiences of people on neuroleptics (and, to some extent, people on antimanics) and people on SSRIs. But there are exceptions. For example, 10 per cent of people on SSRIs tried to come off against their doctors' advice. One woman was on venlafaxine and wanted to come off before she became pregnant. But her psychiatrist said she was being 'very, very silly'. When she went ahead anyway he initially refused to see her.

In the depth interviews, we asked about discrimination to try to find out why people from BME communities tended to have such different experiences of medication from the other participants. We knew that one reason was the far greater proportion of them who were on neuroleptics or antimanics, though why this was so required its own explanation. But what were the other reasons?

Some people gave examples of racism they experienced while using mental health services. For example, one woman talked about how she felt stereotyped as an Asian woman. One aspect of this was how mental health workers felt she should become more independent of her family, assuming the 'Asian-ness' of being involved with the family she was born into was unhealthy. But out of the 14 people from BME communities we interviewed in depth, only one person identified a possible direct link between race and over-prescribing of medication. This woman, who identified as black British, felt misunderstood from when she was first sectioned:

> *It was quite difficult because what I perceived and they perceived were two quite different things. I think there was a lot of misunderstanding. I was diagnosed as bipolar – manic depressive – but I think knowing something about my culture, or even having known something about me, before being diagnosed as manic depressive, would have added light to the real person I am. I just feel that I was brought into the hospital, sectioned; there I was and I needed to fit into a box of other people's preconceived ideas, their assumptions, their medical models, whatever. It was if that was what existed, not me, as someone who has a culture, who has beliefs and her own values.*

She was mystified by the high dose of lithium she was on but when she questioned it the psychiatrist told her it was the right amount for her body weight. But she knew white men who were far heavier but on lower doses of lithium. When asked, in the depth interview, if she thought racism had anything to do with the high dose, she responded:

> *It could be an element of race. It could be because I'm black, maybe black female. It could be an element of fear because there's all this stuff, you know, that black people tend to be over-medicated and you have the more toxic medication given to you. I guess I did fit into that category when I look at it that way.*

Inside Outside: Improving Mental Health Services for Black and Minority Ethnic Communities in England (NIMHE 2003) was the first official policy paper to state that statutory mental health services are institutionally racist (p. 7). It used the definition adopted by Sir William Macpherson (p. 24), who chaired the inquiry into the murder of black teenager, Stephen Lawrence:

> Institutional racism is the collective failure of an organisation to provide an appropriate and professional service to people because of their colour, culture or ethnic origin. It can be seen or detected in processes, attitudes and behaviour which amount to discrimination through unwitting prejudice, ignorance or thoughtlessness and racist stereotyping which disadvantages minority ethnic people.

Perhaps it is institutional racism that best explains the very different experience of medication of people from BME communities compared with the other (non-BME) participants which emerges from the CWCO survey.

5

Coping with Coming Off:
The Consequences

The Experience of Trying to Come off Psychiatric Drugs

We had asked people about their experience of psychiatric drugs and attitudes towards them, why they decided to try to come off them, and how they did or didn't involve their doctors in their decisions. Our next questions were about what happened when they tried to come off. We started by asking how long they took, and the results are shown in Table 5.1.

Nearly a third (32 per cent) of people stopped taking the drugs all at once. We saw in Chapter 3 that anyone who received informed advice would usually have been encouraged to stop more slowly, unless they had only been taking their drugs for a short time.

In the depth interviews, we found a range of reasons why people did come off their drugs in one go. Some people believed or were told that it was fine to do so. Some did so out of necessity. For others it was to do with circumstances, their desire to get off the drugs as soon as possible, or simply a spontaneous decision to stop taking them.

Table 5.1   Over what period people tried to come off their drug(s) (%)

	All	SSRIs	Neuroleptics	Antimanics	BME	Non-BME
All at once, immediately	32	14	39	26	39	30
Less than one month	15	22	12	11	18	14
One to six months	33	51	21	26	26	34
More than six months	21	14	27	37	16	22

One man was on a neuroleptic, an antidepressant and a sleeping pill, and a drug given to people who have abused alcohol to stop them drinking. He tried to get information about coming off from his psychiatrist and a pharmacist, but both refused to speak to him. A friend then told him it was OK just to stop them, and he did. Another man was told by his GP that it was OK to come off lithium in one go.

A woman came off a tranquilliser abruptly partly because it was a long time ago and there wasn't good information around about how to do it, but also she was a teacher; the summer holidays were starting and she hoped to get through withdrawal before the next term. Another woman ran out of her SSRI. She had moved house and it was difficult to get back to her doctor. She had been taking it for months and hadn't experienced any obvious benefit, but was suffering from adverse effects. The difficulty of obtaining a new supply accelerated her decision to stop.

One man was tormented by obsessive thoughts about suicide when on the SSRI sertraline (Lustral) and a neuroleptic for three months:

> *I was having suicidal thoughts non-stop, day and night and it was driving me round the bend. So I'd go to the train station and I'd be feeling like jumping. I felt a force was pushing me and willing me to jump. And when I was asleep at night, I would feel a force pulling me to jump out of the window. And when I went into the kitchen I felt a force urging me to cut my wrists.*

This was in 2001. The patient information leaflet which came with the sertraline said that suicidal thoughts could occur, although it was rare. But the man's psychiatrist wouldn't accept it, saying the symptoms were psychosomatic and a symbolic rejection of the drug. Eventually he came off the drugs without telling anyone, having decided:

> *I cannot spend another day of fighting these suicidal thoughts. I might give into them, if I continue like this.*

The suicidal thoughts ceased as soon as he stopped taking the drugs:

> *I came off and, miraculously, didn't experience any side effects, nothing. And within a day I was fine again.*

One woman was put on several drugs when sectioned in hospital. She didn't even know what they were, but knew she didn't want to be on them. As soon as she was discharged she stopped taking them.

Table 5.2   People who had difficulty trying to come off drug(s) (%)

	All	SSRIs	Neuroleptics	Antimanics	BME	Non-BME
Difficult	60	72	47	50	47	65
Fairly easy	33	25	41	45	53	30
Other	5	3	13	5	0	6

People on neuroleptics and people from BME communities were most likely to have stopped all at once. There is a pattern beginning to develop here. They were also the groups most likely to have come off without their doctors' agreement. Both can be construed as doing 'the wrong thing', acting irresponsibly.

We then asked if people had difficulty coming off their drugs. Table 5.2 shows that 60 per cent did.

People trying to come off SSRIs were significantly more likely to find it difficult than people coming off neuroleptics and antimanics. This is despite them being more likely to come off slowly, as shown in Table 5.1.

People from BME communities were more likely than other people to find coming off their drugs fairly easy: 53 per cent compared with 30 per cent. So despite being more likely to go about it the 'wrong' way, they were more likely to have a fairly easy time. As with other figures showing differences between the experience of people from BME communities and other (non-BME) participants in the survey, some but not all can be explained by more of them coming off a neuroleptic or antimanic.

In Appendix 2, these statistics on difficulty coming off are compared with statistics on unwanted effects when stopping from the *"All you need to know?"* survey (SAMH 2004). Although they differ somewhat, the important information both these surveys provide is that for every psychiatric drug, some people will have difficulties coming off and others won't. But they are more likely to have difficulties coming off some drugs than others. SSRIs top both lists as the drugs most associated with adverse effects when coming off.

We asked people to describe the main difficulties they had in their own words. They covered a vast range of symptoms, including signs of mental distress such as anxiety, depression, hallucinations, mood swings and paranoia. There were symptoms associated with physical illness, including nausea, vomiting and diarrhoea, sweating, a sore throat, and headaches. Some people used the term 'flu-like' symptoms. Disturbed sleep was common.

The most powerful withdrawal reactions came from people coming off tranquillisers and SSRIs. A woman who stopped taking a tranquilliser told us:

My hair fell out, I came out in spots and boils, and I was totally terrified and shocked. I couldn't do anything at all. It just went on and on and on and on. I can't tell you how many horrible effects it had on me.

And a man who also came off a tranquilliser described the last stages of coming off:

During the last week of taking Valium I became almost completely sleepless. I was getting just one or two hours' sleep a night and a terrible thirst all the time. I couldn't drink enough water. Six days after I stopped taking it completely, I had a burning, stinging pain all over my body and severe muscle cramps. On occasions, I got out of bed and fell over. It was so bad. I'd wake up in the night and the lower half of my body would be locked solid.

A woman shared her experience after cutting down to half a tablet of the SSRI paroxetine (Seroxat). For three to five days she was 'high as a kite' and gradually getting headaches. On the fifth day, as she was a qualified nurse she thought she might have meningitis and rang the out-of-hours doctor. The symptoms were so bad, 'I was in absolutely screaming agony with my head; it was as if my brain was trying to get out.' The doctors suggested she should call an ambulance and go to hospital, but before she did so, she decided to take the half-tablet. Within half an hour she was perfectly OK.

A man who had taken and come off a wide variety of psychiatric and street drugs told us that coming off the antidepressant venlafaxine (Efexor) was worse than coming off heroin but not quite as bad as coming off diazepam (a tranquilliser), 'which is in a league of its own'.

The different experiences people can have coming off the same drug are illustrated by looking at what happened to people coming off venlafaxine. One person gave a vivid account of a particular adverse effect which, because venlafaxine has such a short half-life (of five hours), even occurred if she missed a dose:

It's a weird sort of buzzing thing that happens in my head. I liken it to a radio station going off station. You know, when turning the knob of the radio. It's a horrible feeling.

On the internet she found this sensation described as 'brain shivers', which she thought described exactly what it felt like. With people coming off venlafaxine discussing this distinctive symptom on the internet we expected the research to show it to be a common phenomenon. But instead we found that of the 12 other people who tried to come off this drug, only one described a withdrawal effect the same or similar to this. Seven had other difficulties and five came off fairly easily.

Most symptoms associated with coming off drugs are less distinctive than brain shivers and it can be difficult to know what is going on. People can feel anxious, for example, because of distress returning as the effects of the drug wear off, fear about coming off the drug, an effect of withdrawal or a combination of any of these. Other symptoms of coming off can be mistaken for physical illness. Being able to identify the source of these symptoms is crucial as it determines what action to take. Knowing they are part of a withdrawal syndrome which will pass may enable the person to carry on coming off. But if they decide, rightly or wrongly, that they are symptoms of distress, they may decide to go back on the full dose of the drug. Get this wrong and they can spend the rest of their life on a drug they may have been only weeks away from coming off successfully.

One person, coming off a depot injection after more than 20 years, identified an effect that was both difficult and welcome at the same time:

> *It felt strange because I was in touch with emotions – difficult but better than being drugged.*

There were several instances of people coming off neuroleptics having a psychotic episode and ending up back on them. It was difficult for them to know whether or not they were experiencing a withdrawal syndrome. That possibility didn't even occur to some people, who decided this experience showed they needed to be on the drugs. Some who had stopped abruptly concluded that they might have done better by withdrawing more slowly. Generally they were lacking knowledge and support to be able to evaluate their experience and make solid, well-informed decisions about the future.

Next we asked from whom people sought or received help and how useful it was. The results are shown in Table 5.3, with the people most highly rated as very helpful at the top, working down to those least rated as very helpful. It is noticeable that the people with the worst ratings for helpfulness are doctors.

Table 5.3 People seeking and receiving help (%)

	No.	Very helpful	Helpful	Not helpful	Made things worse
Counsellor or psychotherapist	53	53	34	13	0
Support group	52	52	38	8	2
Complementary therapist	39	51	41	8	0
Other service user(s)	81	47	42	7	4
Telephone helpline	42	38	38	21	2
Family member(s)	110	38	35	20	7
Friends (not service users)	100	28	51	16	5
Mental health worker (other than doctor)	76	28	33	33	7
GP	124	13	38	40	10
Psychiatrist	105	12	33	30	24

Table 5.4 People seeking and receiving help from GPs (%)

	No.	Very helpful	Helpful	Not helpful	Made things worse
SSRIs	50	8	46	44	2
Neuroleptics	14	0	36	36	29
Antimanics	10	30	40	30	0
BME	14	0	57	43	0
Non-BME	110	15	35	39	11

The most significant differences between people coming off different types of drugs, and between people from BME communities and others, are in their ratings of doctors. Their ratings of help received from GPs are shown in Table 5.4. Some of the numbers are small because so many people chose not to involve their doctor. They show that people coming off neuroleptics had the most negative experience. No person coming off a neuroleptic rated their GP as very helpful, but 29 per cent said they had made things worse.

Table 5.5 shows how people from these different groupings rated help from psychiatrists, and the same pattern is repeated. They were most negatively rated by people coming off neuroleptics, with 35 per cent saying their psychiatrist made things worse.

People coming off neuroleptics were less likely to tell their doctor than people coming off other drugs and, if they did, were less likely to

Table 5.5   People seeking and receiving help from psychiatrists (%)

	No.	Very helpful	Helpful	Not helpful	Made things worse
SSRIs	27	19	30	26	26
Neuroleptics	20	10	30	25	35
Antimanics	14	36	29	29	7
BME	18	6	39	33	22
Non-BME	7	14	32	30	24

experience them as helpful. There were 33 people coming off a neuroleptic and not any other drug. Of these, 14 sought or received help from their GP and only 5 had a positive experience; 20 sought or received help from a psychiatrist and only 8 had a positive experience.

This contrasts with the experience of people coming off antimanics. We might expect the figures to be similar because those involved face similar issues about compulsion, taking and the notion of drugs for life. But people coming off antimanics were more likely to give their doctors a positive rating. In fact they rated doctors as more helpful than did people coming off SSRIs. The problems people coming off SSRIs had with doctors were often about their refusal to believe there was a withdrawal syndrome. Instead of warning their patients about it, GPS were more likely to refuse to believe them when they reported adverse effects on reducing the dose. One person tried to talk to her consultant about withdrawing from fluoxetine (Prozac). This was in the 1990s. She told us:

> I told the consultant I just wanted to come off Prozac and he said, 'Well, just stop.' And I said, 'I've been reading about it and I understand that it's not a very safe thing to do.' And he replied, 'There's absolutely no evidence to show it's a problem and all you have to do is just stop. If there's a problem it will be because of your depression and not because of the drug.'

Obviously, as the prescribers of psychiatric drugs, doctors should be the main source of help, support and advice about coming off them, even though that advice might be 'don't do it'. For them to be rated so poorly, something is going badly wrong. Our analysis of the depth interviews suggested the following differences between doctors and their patients. Doctors were seen as:

- more likely to see drugs as beneficial;
- less concerned about adverse effects;

- less likely to understand the desire to live without them;
- more likely to doubt the ability of the patient to manage without them (especially neuroleptics and antimanics);
- less likely to value alternative and complementary strategies and sources of help and support;
- more likely to underestimate the difficulties of withdrawal (especially from SSRIs).

Additionally, doctors were often not well-informed about withdrawal syndromes or the best methods of coming off drugs. Either that or they chose not to share this information with their patients. There were, for example, instances of doctors erroneously telling patients that lower doses of their drugs were not available. One person was told by her psychiatrist that venlafaxine was not available in doses lower than a 75mg capsule, which is the recommended starting dose. Consequently, in order to taper her withdrawal, she was taking them on alternate days. Because venlafaxine has such a short half-life (of five hours) she would have been going in and out of withdrawal. She later found out she could have been prescribed 37.5mg tablets, which she could then have divided.

Even when doctors warned people to come off their drugs slowly, they rarely gave them any information about what withdrawal symptoms they might expect or discussed with them how to adjust to life without the drugs.

The most illuminating quotes about doctors are those which contrast unhelpful attitudes and behaviour with more positive responses. One man described a psychiatrist as very authoritarian:

> *His attitude was, 'We're doing all this work for you and it's costing the NHS a fortune, and you're not cooperating.' There was an element of coercion in it.*

But he found another psychiatrist:

> *...brilliant, really. He said, 'If you don't want to take the drugs, don't take them. We'll work around it and, if you're not taking them, we can observe things in the raw. We can try drama therapy and whatever else.'*

A young woman contrasted the attitudes of two GPs. Of the first, she said:

> *The doctor didn't have time, didn't understand the issue and didn't really want to. He was happy to dish out the drugs but I couldn't talk to him because he didn't want to know.*

When interviewed, she was with a new GP who was supporting her to come off paroxetine (Seroxat):

My current GP is great. I can talk stuff through with her and she's very informed on issues and has said she's not actually prescribing Seroxat to new patients.

A man who had taken several different drugs contrasted the attitudes of two doctors towards giving information:

I remember asking a psychiatrist on one occasion what the side effects of an antidepressant he was prescribing me were and he said, 'We don't generally tell people any of the side effects. They might imagine them.'

His GP was:

...totally different, really. He gave me this leaflet all about lithium and said 'You read this and you'll know just as much as I do.'

This person also gave an example of the resistance some doctors have to patients coming off their drugs:

Another one said to me that I'd be on lithium the rest of my life. If I ever went off it my friends and family would tell me to go back on it. They'd notice that I was behaving differently.

When interviewed, he hadn't taken a psychiatric drug for more than ten years.

Other people were rated more highly than doctors for the help they provided. But this help was rarely specifically about the details of how to come off drugs. Instead, it tended to fall into one or more of these categories:

- encouragement, belief in the person and personal support;
- the opportunity to be listened to non-judgmentally and helped to think things through;
- understanding of and belief in alternative approaches to the medical model.

One woman described the assistance she received from a psycho-therapist. With him she was able to look at and work through her fears of what might happen when she came off lithium – fears of losing insight and ending up back on a psychiatric ward. Although she didn't recall her therapist saying he agreed or disagreed with her decision, she felt supported by him and that he was confident in her ability to handle it.

Another spoke of the benefits of getting involved in her local service users' group:

> *I was meeting people who were coming off their medication and were saying, 'Yes, it's possible, you can do it.' And so I was building up a support network informally to help me.*

Others felt supported by family and friends:

> *A lot of my close family and friends see that I've got strength and I don't need to be on the drug.*

Critical Reflection Box 5.1

Nurses Prescribing Psychiatric Drugs

Doctors are rated poorly for their attitudes and skills in helping people who want to try coming off psychiatric drugs, but would nurses do better? Although nurses in the UK can qualify to prescribe drugs, mental health nurses have been reluctant to do so. (See, for example, Snowden 2008.) Being a prescriber isn't necessary to take on a role of offering support and advice to people wanting to come off their drugs, but having that power does grant additional authority, autonomy and opportunity.

This exercise asks you to reflect on the advantages and disadvantages of nurses prescribing psychiatric drugs by responding to the following questions:

1. What do you think are the advantages and disadvantages to nurses in becoming prescribers of psychiatric drugs, considering such matters as career advancement and job satisfaction?
2. What do you think are the advantages and disadvantages to service users of nurses becoming prescribers of psychiatric drugs, taking into account the key issues of choice and compulsion?
3. Do you think suitably trained nurses can do a better job of prescribing psychiatric drugs than doctors? What are the reasons for your answer?
4. Taking your responses to the previous three questions into account, would you welcome a significant expansion of prescribing by mental health nurses?

Once the internet became readily available it became a source of information and support to people trying to come off psychiatric drugs. Table 5.6 shows that about a quarter of the people we interviewed made use of the internet or email groups. Many of the participants came off their drugs before the internet was created or before it became relatively easy to access or, no doubt, a higher proportion would have used it.

The value of the internet is vividly illustrated by the story of a doctor who was coming off fluoxetine (Prozac) in 2001. Having reduced the dose gradually, it was only when she stopped completely that she started to feel there was something wrong:

> *The overriding memory is of trying to have conversations with people and feeling my head was made of cotton wool. And I found it incredibly difficult to get my thoughts together and concentrate on what I was doing. And my memory was atrocious. And driving, I found my reaction times were much slower and I just couldn't seem to get it together. I felt completely out of it, which made me think I was getting depressed again. And I was actually quite concerned there was something physically wrong or metabolically wrong.*

At the time, most of her medical colleagues and the medical press were not recognising there was a withdrawal syndrome and it was only when one colleague drew her attention to a website set up by and for people who had experienced difficulties coming off SSRIs that she found the information which made a crucial difference to her:

> *I looked up the symptoms on the internet and that was exactly what I was experiencing. And it gave me the confidence to say, 'Well if that's all it is it will wear off and I'll just progress through it.' But I was within a hare's whisker of taking Prozac again because it was so unbearable.*

Table 5.6 shows that accessing the internet and email groups was the activity or approach most highly rated as very helpful. But it was far more likely to be used by people coming off SSRIs (49 per cent) than people coming off neuroleptics (18 per cent) or antimanics (15 per cent). Good sources of information on coming off drugs were scarce (most of those listed in Appendix 1 were not available when this research was carried out), and especially so for people coming off neuroleptic or antimanics.

Table 5.6   The helpfulness of activities and approaches (%)

	No.	Very helpful	Helpful	Not helpful	Made things worse
The internet and email groups	54	43	52	6	0
Exercise	115	39	51	9	1
Creative activity	94	39	49	12	0
Spirituality or religion	82	39	48	12	1
Books or other written information	123	37	54	7	2
Major lifestyle changes	68	35	49	12	4
Relaxation or meditation	88	30	63	8	0
Herbal remedies	43	28	51	16	5
Dietary changes	49	20	59	18	2
Social drugs, e.g. alcohol, cannabis	57	7	35	26	32

The other activities and approaches were mainly about finding alternatives to a strictly medical model. This included books and other written information. One person who experienced depression, anxiety and panic attacks was particularly enthusiastic about self-help books. He was feeling that he may have to go back on his drugs but, instead, decided to visit his local bookshop. He told us:

I was surprised to learn how many self-help books there were dealing with this sort of problem. And it was then I realised that this is a big problem, a common problem. It's not just me. There must be millions of us, because if people are stocking these books they must be making money out of them. Surprisingly enough, when I asked the chap about the books he was quite helpful and pointed me to the books I ought to have. I even thought, 'Next time I won't go to the doctor, I'll go down to Waterstones.'

We were interested to see that major lifestyle changes were generally rated as helpful. Advice about coming off drugs often includes the suggestion that it is best to do it when your life is relatively quiet and stable. But we found there were people who decided to re-evaluate their lives and make a fresh start. For them, coming off their drugs was part of a process they had initiated themselves, of taking charge of their lives. The change and upheaval were helpful and could even provide a welcome distraction, as one woman explained.

She had been the financial director of a large organisation and was advised by her doctor not to go back to her job, which she accepted: 'Part of my sickness was that I was quite paranoid about the extent to which the people I had been working with had made me mad.' She decided, instead, to enrol on a college course, which necessitated moving across the country. She had been struggling to get off the SSRI, paroxetine, but was stuck on half a tablet every third day. She was determined to take the last step before she began her course, and told us:

> in all the kerfuffle of moving – if you can imagine moving a household and a cat – I had to put the cat in a cattery, then move, then go back for the cat – I suddenly realised I hadn't taken a tablet for a week and I hadn't got any worse than I had been on day three of my previous attempt. So I've never taken one since.

Activities and approaches such as exercise and creativity were found to be useful by most people who tried them. Although we were asking about them in the context of coming off drugs, their value was broader than that. They were evaluated similarly positively in the *Knowing Our Own Minds* research (see Table 2.3).

Factors which Influenced Success

Having tried to come off psychiatric drugs, some people succeeded and others didn't. In this section we look at what factors influenced success. We didn't try to define success. We left it to the people we interviewed to make their own judgements about themselves. Clearly, having come off the drug(s) was a starting point. But how successful people rated themselves as also depended on how long they had stayed off the drug and how well they had managed without it. People who said they were partially successful may have succeeded in reducing but not coming off completely, may have gone back on a different drug that suited them better, or may have gone back on the same drug but been pleased to have had a break from it. Some people hadn't succeeded, and others were still trying to come off and were not yet able to say how successful they were.

We deliberately chose a sample of people to interview of whom about half had completely succeeded. So we cannot say from this survey what proportion of people who try to come off their drugs succeed. But we can see how various factors influenced success.

Table 4.1 showed the breakdown of different levels of success of all the participants. For this section we have excluded the people for whom coming off was still ongoing. Of the rest, 53 per cent said they had completely succeeded.

Table 5.7 shows the degree of success of people from different categories. It is interesting to see that people from BME groups were the most likely to succeed, given that they were also the least compliant group (see Table 4.8), But not too much should be made of small differences in success. Basically, the table shows that what type of drug participants were coming off or whether they were from a BME community or not made little difference to success. People coming off the drugs which are most often seen as 'drugs for life' were roughly as likely to succeed as people coming off SSRIs, which are usually prescribed for a more limited time.

Table 5.8 shows how much the length of time people had been on their drug influenced their success in coming off. It made a significant difference. These figures strongly suggest that the longer you take psychiatric drugs for, the harder it is to come off them. Many people who tried coming off their drugs didn't do so in the most careful and controlled way. This probably mattered less for people who hadn't been on them so long. The lesson from these findings is probably that, the longer you have been on your drugs, the more thoughtful you need to be about how you approach trying to come off them.

Table 5.9 shows that how the doctor was or wasn't involved in the decision to try coming off made little difference to success. People who

Table 5.7 Success in coming off

	Those completely successful (%)
All	53
SSRIs	56
Neuroleptics	52
Antimanics	61
BME	62
Non-BME	51

Table 5.8 How long on the drug

	Those completely successful (%)*
Less than a year	75
One to five years	55
More than five years	42

*People coming off a single drug.

Table 5.9   How the decision to try coming off drug(s) was made

	Those completely successful (%)
Decided against advice of doctor	50
Decided without telling doctor	54
I decided and my doctor accepted	40
Joint decision between me and my doctor	56
My doctor decided and I accepted	41
Other	52

Table 5.10   How fast people came off the drug

	Those completely successful (%)*
All at once, immediately	59
Less than one month	67
One to six months	61
More than six months	59

*People coming off a single drug.

came off against their doctor's advice or without telling their doctor were as likely to succeed as people whose doctors were involved in the decision. Most of the people who avoided telling their doctor did so because they didn't expect their doctor to agree with their decision. People in these two categories can be considered to be non-compliant. This finding challenges the notion of compliance and non-compliance, with its implications that people should always follow their doctor's instructions. It suggests that doctors cannot easily predict who can safely come off their drugs.

Table 5.10 shows how the length of time people took to come off their drug influenced their success in coming off. It made little obvious difference. This appears to contradict advice that it is best to come off slowly. There are probably three factors that explain this discrepancy. First, some people are able to come off their drugs easily, regardless of how fast they do it. Secondly, it tends to be easier coming off them if you haven't been on them long. It is likely that a relatively high proportion of people who came off all at once had not been taking their drugs for long. We know from Table 5.8 that the less time you have been taking your drugs the more likely you are to succeed in coming off them. Thirdly, some people who started coming off fast and ran into difficulties then went back on to their original dose and came off more slowly. In those instances, coming off slowly was a consequence of running into difficulties.

We took out some of the variables, and looked at the experience of people coming off an SSRI who had been on it between one and five years. Of those who tried to come off in less than a month, four out of ten succeeded. Of those who took one to six months, ten out of sixteen succeeded. The numbers are small but do suggest that coming off slowly is still the best option.

Learning from Experience

People's attempts to come off their drugs resulted in varying degrees of success. Some started but felt unable to continue. They were not always sure if their difficulties were a withdrawal syndrome, distress re-emerging as they came off their drugs, or if there was some other explanation. Others came off their medication but went back on it again or went on to another drug. If this turned out to be a better one for them, their efforts hadn't been wasted. Some people were making slow progress towards coming off and were hopeful of eventually succeeding. Others had succeeded in coming off and staying off their drugs, although some were prepared to go back on them if they thought it necessary.

We were interested to see if people who hadn't succeeded felt there was anything positive about having tried or whether it was simply a negative experience. We found there were useful lessons people felt they could take from their experiences.

Some people thought they had probably failed because they didn't think through what they were doing. This left them with the option of trying again. One man had spontaneously come off a neuroleptic all at once and ended up back on it. Thinking about whether he would try again, he told us:

> If I'm going to do it at all, it's going to be piecemeal, in stages and it has to be done with a consortium of experts and not just be a one-man show.

There was another group who felt they had learned that they needed to be on their drugs. One man who had been on an SSRI for several years came off it in about a month. He didn't experience any ill effects at the time, but soon after became severely depressed and went back on it. He said:

> The experiment was successful to the extent that it emphasised the need for some antidepressant medication.

But, as researchers, we were left with the uneasy feeling that some of the people who reached this conclusion about themselves may have been going through a withdrawal syndrome without realising it.

Some people were left unsure, such as this woman who didn't succeed in coming off venlafaxine:

> *My question to myself, which is unanswerable, is that perhaps I'd be this way if I was on the drugs or not, and the only difficulty is the withdrawal problem. Maybe I'd be exactly like this if I was not on them. But I just can't seem to get past the barrier.*

Some people decided it was time to pursue other objectives. One woman told us:

> *I wasn't successful in coming off the medication but I think I was successful in coming to some realisation that for me personally – and obviously it isn't the same for everybody else – but for me personally it wasn't such a major deal. It was a nice idea if I could come off but there were too many other things that were a problem to me that I was better off spending my energy working on...I made this discovery with [my psychotherapist] that I could actually explore things that I really liked. I am trying to give myself permission to do things that are just for me and not everybody else.*

Other people were struggling to deal with the disappointment and find a way forward. One man had reduced the dose of his neuroleptic slowly, but when he stopped taking it completely ended up in hospital and back on it. Thinking about his desire to be off his medication, he told us:

> *It puts a lot of pressure on me to fulfil my dreams of being clear...a huge amount of pressure on me. I could take the pressure off by just accepting. It almost forces you into resignation of taking medication the rest of your life...and that might be where you get your peace. To get the peace of being is to resign yourself to this fate of medication, because there's no other option.*

But he went on to say:

> *I'm still hopeful that I'll self-heal and won't need them. I'm still hopeful that the psychotherapy I have and the support I have around me and the work I do on myself will be enough to recover to the state that I won't have a mental health problem. I will have knitted my mind back together.*

He also thought about what would help him and others in his predicament:

> *By now, the recovered people should have been studied and there should be homes set up according to their models. How they came off should have been analysed and people should have learned from it.*

He finished by suggesting:

> *It's almost as if there's a sort of disbelief about recovery. Maybe there's not any money in it.*

Celebrating Success

Some people who succeeded in coming off their drugs expressed reservations about their achievements because they were left struggling in some way. But most were effusive about the benefits. It was striking that some people gave their main benefit of being off them as improved mental health – what you might expect people to say about the benefits of going on to psychiatric drugs. Take this man who stopped taking tranquillisers:

> *My beaten-up car goes for its MOT in January every year and, when I was taking the medication, I used to stand there watching every single move the mechanics were making, listening to every little squeak. But after I stopped taking the medication, I just took it round there, went away and came back again – quite a difference.*

Specific improvements to mental health mentioned by more than one person were being more motivated to do things; more sociable and outgoing; less depressed or suicidal; more creative; more optimistic; and sleeping better.

The most commonly mentioned benefits were: having my life back; feeling more alive and human; better concentration, alertness, memory and mental ability; the absence of adverse effects; and a sense of self-determination, having taken back power and control.

One man had been put on a neuroleptic in the 1950s. He must have been one of the first people to take these drugs. He had several hospital admissions. Each time he was put on chlorpromazine and told to stay on it for life, and each time he stopped taking it as soon as he could. He was motivated by his own reaction to the drug – feeling it was taking away his thinking abilities – and seeing other patients in the hospital 'turning into zombies'. Meanwhile, through reading books by people such as Freud and Jung, he was trying to work out how to integrate the different aspects of his personality, as he believed his breakdowns were caused by them being in conflict.

He had to hide his coming off the drugs from his family, who were instructed by the doctor to make sure he took them. This wasn't easy, as he would feel more intolerant and his temper would show more. But he would also enjoy:

> *A feeling of great exhilaration, a feeling of getting my power back and being able to do things I couldn't do before.*

Eventually, his own self-help methods worked. He stayed off his medication and out of hospital. He was able to have a successful career and, when interviewed, had not taken psychiatric drugs for 35 years.

Some people spoke of 'being more myself'. A young woman who came off an antidepressant against her doctor's advice said:

> *I feel more like myself. I feel I am finally finding myself. Because I started on this medication when I was 17 and I just tried to change myself to fit with other people by taking this medication and, now I'm off it, I'm starting to actually be myself.*

A woman who came off lithium was also pleased to be free of the routine of drug-taking:

> *I didn't like this relationship with the tablet. While I was on lithium I never quite knew where my emotions were and how much they were being affected by lithium, and so, without it, I felt free of that and could be in touch with my whole emotional self. And there is just that reality of living on medication. If you go away, you always have to take enough with you. It's very much the practicalities of it. If you do something spontaneous you might not have it with you, or you might have forgotten to take it and then you might not remember if you have or haven't taken it. These are the little details that are really huge when you're taking medication and which are fantastic not to have to think about.*

Being able to feel more isn't always pleasant or easy but may still be welcome. This woman, who came off fluoxetine after five or six years.

summed up life without it:

> *It's hard to control my appetite again, but never mind. [Laughs.] So I miss that. What's it like not being on Prozac? I think it's always scary when you're not on your antidepressants because you could always go down again. And I think not having them in the background; I mean it's been great to be able to feel again. I think I found a lot of my emotions were quite numb and I actually feel a lot more able to experience things like sadness and joy...So although, generally, my overall mood was better, I don't think I experienced a full range of human emotion and it's great now to be able to cry at a soppy film again, which I haven't done for years. So that's good.*
>
> *What's it like being off them? I mean I had my scare when there was a life event happened and I got low and thought it was depression and was able to come out of it. I think you probably need to do that when you come off antidepressants, just to experience a real low rather than a depressive low. I think that helps to alleviate your fear, when you finally do come out of it on your own without the use of pills.*

Critical Reflection Box 5.2

Competing Views, Priorities and Responsibilities

Mental health workers can find themselves caught up in conflict between competing views, priorities and responsibilities. These may come from their own professional judgement, the multidisciplinary team, more senior workers and the service users.

You are a member of a community-based multidisciplinary team, but not a doctor. Here are two dilemmas which raise issues about shared decision-making and adherence to consider:

1. Errol is a black man who was diagnosed with bipolar disorder three years ago. Since the initial episode that brought him to the attention of mental health services he has been prescribed the SGN, olanzapine. Although his mental state and behaviour have been quite stable he also seems stuck, doing very little with his life. He has put on some weight, which he is unhappy about, and complains of feeling listless.

   Several times he has complained to you about his medication and you have encouraged him to talk to the psychiatrist who prescribes it. On this occasion he says he told the psychiatrist he wanted to come off it but the psychiatrist said he needs to take it for several more years or there is a high probability he will relapse. Errol tells you he thinks the psychiatrist, who is white, is being racist because he doesn't listen and

COPING WITH COMING OFF: THE CONSEQUENCES **135**

doesn't seem to care that he is wasting his life away. He asks you, as another black person, to support him to explain to the psychiatrist that medication shouldn't be used to subdue him.

It occurs to you that you could say to Errol that he has the right to stop taking his medication, that he may not relapse, especially if he comes off it slowly and that, anyway, he might have a relapse if he stays on it. What do you do?

2. Judith was diagnosed with schizophrenia many years ago and is on the FGN, sulpiride. On several occasions she has stopped taking it and ended up being sectioned. You know her well but she has never been forthcoming about why she does this, just saying things such as, 'I was fed up with it.' From what you have observed you don't see these occasions in a negative light. She seems to have several days of being much more alive than usual before things spiral out of control and seems to feel quite at home on the hospital ward, perhaps enjoying the break from her usual rather solitary existence. But as the most junior member of the team you haven't felt able to share these thoughts, and they expect you to ensure she is taking her medication.

When you visit her she is more animated than usual and can't focus on one subject for any length of time. She insists that she is taking her medication but you are not convinced.

(a) How do you respond to the situation?

(b) Can you see a way of changing Judith's relationship with medication for the better?

6
Coping with Coming Off: Three Stories

Introduction

One theme that emerges from the CWCO research concerns people on neuroleptics and, to a lesser extent, antimanics, and the basis on which they make decisions to come off their drugs. In particular, how do they relate to doctors and other mental health workers about their decision making, and why?

We have seen that people who tried coming off neuroleptics and antimanics were more likely than people coming off other types of drugs to rate the ones they had taken as mainly harmful (Table 4.4). Most had been compelled to take medication under mental health legislation and often had experiences of coercion, powerlessness and passivity in relation to decisions about taking them (Table 4.5).

Their most common reasons for wanting to come off neuroleptics and antimanics were not liking the adverse effects and not liking the idea of being on them long term. Half of people on antimanics and nearly a quarter of those on neuroleptics were not finding their drugs useful (Table 4.6).

Around half the people on neuroleptics and antimanics decided to come off them against their doctors' advice or without telling their doctor (Table 4.8). In the language of doctors and legislators, they were being non-compliant. People on these types of drugs who did seek or receive help from doctors about coming off their drugs rated them lower than any other people from whom they sought or received help (Table 5.3).

These findings could simply be taken as evidence of an age-old and inevitable conflict between doctors, other mental health workers and people diagnosed with what, these days, is called severe mental illness. Patients need their drugs; because they are ill they don't realise this; they stop taking the drugs; they get ill again; mental health services have to step in and rescue the situation for the safety and well-being of the patient and society; and so it goes on.

But this perspective is challenged by some further findings. First of all, people trying to come off these drugs were as likely to succeed as people coming off other psychiatric drugs not so strongly associated with the same debates about lack of insight, non-compliance and the need for compulsion (Table 5.7). Secondly, people who went against their doctor's advice or didn't tell their doctor they were trying to come off were as likely to succeed as those who did. Table 5.9 shows this for all participants in the survey. By combining categories, we can come up with a meaningful figure specifically for people coming off neuroleptics or antimanics.

Table 6.1 shows that 58 per cent of the people who were non-compliant (went against their doctor's advice or didn't tell their doctor) succeeded compared with 50 per cent of the people who were compliant (all other categories). These figures suggest something is going wrong; that doctors are being too conservative in wanting to keep people on these drugs.

Within the depth interviews is a wealth of information about the negotiations people undertook, or tried to undertake, with their doctors and other mental health workers about coming off these drugs. To bring out the complexities and subtleties of how people reach decisions about wanting to come off, what they do and do not communicate with mental health professionals and why, and how they go about withdrawing, three people's stories are presented here. They are based on the original depth interviews, carried out in 2004, with some additions and updating.

It was not our original intention to use the interviews in this way. We appreciate the contribution of these three people in agreeing to their stories appearing here. Although their names have been changed and some details omitted, they are aware that there is potentially some loss of confidentiality involved in having their stories published in such detail. These particular stories have been chosen because between them they cover many of the issues that arise from the CWCO research, as they affect people on neuroleptic and antimanic medication.

Table 6.1 Rate of success for people coming off a neuroleptic or antimanic

	No.	Those who succeeded (%)
Non-compliant	26	58
Compliant	24	50
Total	*50*	*54*

Critical Reflection Box 6.1

Learning from Service Users

1. When reading each of these accounts, and before you get to the comments that follow each of them, jot down any learning points for you personally.
2. Review these learning points when you reach the end of the chapter and complete the following statements:

   (a) The most significant lesson for me from this chapter is...
   (b) My biggest challenge in taking this into my practice is...
   (c) One step I can take is...

Brenda's Story: Coming off Lithium with Support

Brenda was first diagnosed with bipolar disorder in 1995 and started taking lithium and an SSRI. They didn't work well and she had three brief hospital admissions that year, one following an overdose. She was tried on carbamazepine, which proved to be ineffective. The neuroleptic, haloperidol, produced unacceptable adverse effects and she had a dangerous allergic reaction to another, chlorpromazine. In 1996 she asked to go back on the lithium, which she took until 2003. During this time she tried a third neuroleptic, olanzapine, which only added to the weight gain she was experiencing from the lithium. She then went on to sodium valproate as well, which she was still taking when she was interviewed, although she didn't think it was doing her much good.

Although she had not thought the lithium was helping her, prior to 2002, she hadn't got far when she talked to psychiatrists about coming off it. She described her first psychiatrist as 'one of the old school'. Their relationship wasn't helped by his insistence that she had manic depressive psychosis, whereas she didn't agree that there was a psychotic element to her distress:

I found his attitude extremely depressing. He never gave me any grounds for hope or optimism. He never suggested psychotherapy or anything else to help and he made me feel I was going to be stuck out of work and on medication and just about mumbling through the rest of my life and was 41 at the time and I'd had a very busy job and other things in my life until then.

She has rapid-cycling manic depression and continued to go high and low quite regularly while taking medication.

While on the lithium her weight escalated from 10st 12lb to 18st 6lb, which affected her confidence and self-image. Other adverse effects included not being able to concentrate, think clearly or remember things as well as she was used to; feeling sluggish and tired; and sometimes a tingling sensation in her arms and legs. She also talked of sometimes feeling 'kind of separated from everyday things'.

Prior to her attempt to come off lithium she had benefited greatly from her involvement in a local bipolar self-help group, which she now helps to run. She was assisted and inspired by a woman who explained self-management to her:

> *It was more encouraging than even reading about it. And she was doing it – self-managing – using some medication but varying what she took and taking great care of herself in terms of rest, diet, pacing, exercise and all this. I saw the light at the end of the tunnel. In speaking to her I realised that it was possible to stand up and say, 'I don't want this medication you know, I think it's not helping me.'*

She did a lot of reading, finding out about what could help her, such as aromatherapy, meditation and exercise. She learned about 'mind/food stuff': the benefits of Omega 3, 6 and 9 and B vitamins and minerals, and the need to keep a steady blood-sugar level before coming off lithium.

Eventually she decided she was ready to try coming off lithium. She hoped to gain the support of her GP and psychiatrist, but was prepared to go ahead without this, if necessary.

She had a good relationship with her GP. When she told him what she was planning to do his initial reaction was one of some puzzlement and surprise. He told her that lithium was a safe drug to be on and that people didn't always realise it was helping them. But when he saw she was going to involve the psychiatrist and wanted to come off gradually and be supervised while she did so, he relaxed and became supportive.

She was surprised and pleased by the reaction of her psychiatrist – no longer the man who had been 'one of the old school':

> *I feel I was lucky with her and she was open-minded, although she hadn't encouraged me with this before when I'd thrown the idea at her. That's interesting, isn't it? I think I must have had to prove that I'd learnt enough to make changes to the medication.*

It was December 2002 and Brenda had had a traumatic year. Her psychiatrist suggested Brenda should see her again in January and, if she still wanted to go ahead, she would support her. She wanted them to agree a contract about how Brenda's moods would be monitored and suggested that she investigated exercise and weight loss, warning her that the weight wouldn't come off easily just through stopping the lithium.

Brenda found the proposal of a contract helpful. When she went back she had drawn up a draft version for the psychiatrist, her Community Psychiatric Nurse and her GP. It was basically about staying in touch with them and together monitoring her mood as she came off the lithium. With a couple of minor changes, they agreed it. She said:

> *I felt the power base shifted enormously when I started saying to her, 'This is what I want to do. I can't see a problem with it providing I'm careful, and I'm willing to go back on it if necessary – if I believe or you believe or the GP believes that things are slipping.'*

She added:

> *It was like a train and, instead of being five carriages back, and they* [the doctors] *were in the driving seat at the front, I felt that we were sitting side by side.*

By this time, Brenda felt well-supported in her decision. Her husband was very supportive as he knew she didn't feel well on lithium and wasn't happy about taking it. Her Christian faith was a help to her and a lay worker in the Methodist church she belonged to said she could ring him at any time. She'd gleaned a lot of information from people who had come off the drug, and not in a controlled way, but had said, 'I did it. I made my mind up to do it and I've done it and I'm no worse for it.' It gave her the confidence to get past the medical view of 'I wouldn't do it if I were you; you don't know how much worse you'll be.'

Brenda described her thoughts as she started coming off:

> *I always tried to keep an open mind whilst hoping against hope that I didn't have to go back on the lithium. I always tried to say that if I have to, then I do, because being well is more important than being drug-free.*

She didn't experience any adverse effects as she gradually came off the drug:

> *I felt enormously pleased that I was down from one step to the next over a short period of time, that I was making headway. I did experience, within a very short period of time, an increase in my mental acuity. I just felt like I got my brain back. That was enormously helpful and empowering.*

She was off lithium in a month and, by then, was already beginning to lose weight.

Looking back on the experience, she told us that she felt lithium had not contributed to her well-being and she wished she had come off it earlier:

> *It would have spared me some of the misery of the self-image and all the other problems that go with going up six to eight dress sizes, and the physical problems that go with it, including the worsening of* [pre-existing] *back and joint pains.*

Brenda lost two stone in her first year off lithium. But life without lithium wasn't straightforward because she continued to have mood swings. She was taking sleeping pills occasionally. She said research showed that people with bipolar disorder need at least six or seven hours' sleep. In the past, she might have sat up all night reading or writing. She added:

> *I might allow myself a 24-hour period where I'm pretty high before I say to myself, 'start marking the chart, girl'.*

She was thinking seriously about coming off the sodium valproate. She finished by saying of coming off drugs:

> *I just wish people in general had an awareness that it is their right, their privilege and their choice to try coming off.*

When she was contacted again in 2007 Brenda said that, in some respects, she hadn't made the progress she had hoped. She was still taking sodium valproate. She had also tried the neuroleptic quetiapine, but experienced severe nausea and hives – swellings on her face, hands and feet. But she said:

> *Although I still have mood swings which can be scary and I had hoped would be less frequent, I am still glad I came off lithium. I think the*

'chemical overcoat' effect I experienced while on it probably made me feel less sensitive or anxious than I sometimes feel now, but I wouldn't trade having to cope with those feelings for being back on lithium and feeling less alive.

She thought the way forward was to take greater care with self-management and to continue to seek out information and knowledge. She thanked the people who had helped her in her journey to 'find the real "me" previously defined by the label of bipolar'.

COMMENT ON BRENDA'S STORY

Brenda stayed on lithium for seven years, even though it didn't seem to be working and there were serious adverse effects. Of course, she could not be sure of what would happen if she stopped, and neither could her psychiatrist. No one knows what will happen when someone stops taking their drugs. They could be better off, worse off or stay the same. There is always an element of experiment and the uncertainty can make patients and doctors cautious about trying it.

There is an evident contrast between Brenda's experiences of the two psychiatrists. It doesn't sound as if her first one would have been willing to support her decision to come off. Contrasting experiences of different doctors was common for people who participated in the CWCO survey. Positive experiences of doctors demonstrate that conflict isn't inevitable, but some people are missing out on opportunities to try coming off their drugs with the support of their doctor, simply because they have the wrong doctor.

Even though none of the drugs Brenda had taken over more than nine years to the time of the interview had controlled her rapid-cycling mood swings, she was not offered any alternative approaches by statutory services. It was through the Manic Depressive Fellowship (now called MDF The BiPolar Organisation) that she came across the concept of self-management which gave her another perspective. But, like all such organisations, its funding and networks are patchy. Many people with this diagnosis are unlikely to encounter these ideas or find an active group easily accessible to them. (There were just over one hundred MDF self-help groups in England in 2007.)

The problem with matching drugs with diagnoses and assuming they will work is that there isn't a 'Plan B'. Perhaps, on an unconscious level, psychiatrists are reluctant to take people off drugs which are not being effective because then they will be seen to be offering nothing.

Brenda was a model of assertiveness. She made it easy for her psychiatrist. But why should she have had to handle her situation so well? Most people, whether recipients of psychiatric services or not, do not have her mix of confidence, tact, communication skills and determination.

For Brenda, the challenge was getting to the point of being determined to try coming off the lithium. Actually coming off was easy, even though she had been taking it continuously for seven years. But another person coming off lithium might have had a quite different experience. One of the strong lessons from this research is that you can be prepared for what might happen when you try coming off psychiatric drugs, but the only way of finding out is to try it.

Although she thinks she is probably more sensitive and anxious without the lithium, on balance, Brenda is still pleased to have stopped taking it. With psychiatric drugs decisions are often not clear-cut. They are made 'on balance' – and often balancing different factors such as long-term physical health against short-term symptom reduction.

Stephen's Story: Coming off Sulpiride Slowly

Stephen first developed mental health problems after the shock of finding his twin brother dead from heart failure, aged 34. He became depressed and was put on the tricyclic antidepressant, dosulepin (Prothiaden). He stopped taking it and later was admitted to hospital where he was put on another tricyclic, imipramine (Tofranil). This was in 2000.

After he was discharged he started smoking a lot of cannabis – up to 20 joints a day. In 2001–2 he was admitted to hospital on three further occasions. Each time he was high and psychotic when admitted, but stabilised soon after being put on psychiatric drugs and ceasing to smoke cannabis. He suspected that the effects of smoking cannabis may have been his biggest problem. The drugs he was on included the SSRI sertraline (Lustral) at one stage.

On one occasion he had an immediate and serious reaction to the neuroleptic, haloperidol, and couldn't stop his tongue protruding. He was given an injection of an anti-Parkinson's drug.

One psychiatrist diagnosed him with manic depression and told him he should take lithium. But he resisted. When interviewed, he recalled this exchange of views:

Psychiatrist: *You've got manic depression.*

Stephen: *I still think it might be the cannabis.*

Psychiatrist: *Well, we don't think it is. We think you have actually got manic depression and if you are smoking it, it's because you've got manic depression.*

Stephen: *Well, I don't think so.*

Psychiatrist: *Well, we think so.*

He came under a lot of pressure from staff in the hospital to take lithium but continued to refuse. He was taking the neuroleptic, sulpiride, but tried coming off it over a few weeks and ended up back in hospital for the fourth and last time, in 2002. He went back on the sulpiride but would not agree to take the antimanic, sodium valproate. He started on 400mg of sulpiride twice a day and negotiated to have it reduced to 200mg twice a day. Soon after being discharged he cut it, first to 200mg in the day and 100mg at night and then to 100mg twice a day.

Stephen also made several important decisions about living his life better and about coming off and staying off his medication. He stopped smoking cannabis. It meant breaking off contact with his friends. He signed up for a couple of adult education classes and joined a gardening project for people diagnosed as mentally ill. But life was tough; he was spending a lot of time on his own – 'my partner was working long hours to support us both' – and he didn't feel good a lot of the time, but was still pleased with his progress.

He continued to be in conflict with his psychiatrist and recalls a conversation at an outpatients' appointment that went something like this:

Psychiatrist: *You will be ill again. It's not if, it's when.*

Stephen: *I don't want to hear this.*

Psychiatrist: *Well, it's going to happen, and you need to take something like sodium valproate.*

Stephen: *Well, OK, but if I do take it can you guarantee I will be well for ever?*

Psychiatrist: *Well, no.*

Stephen: *I'm not interested, then. Unless I really need it and you can prove it is going to do me good, long term, and I'm not going to be ill, then I'm not going to take it. I'm stable on sulpiride, so why do I need a mood stabiliser?*

Psychiatrist: *To flatten your moods out.*

Stephen: *Well, they're OK, so why do I want them flat and level, because that isn't normal, is it?*

Psychiatrist: *If you've got manic depression…*

Stephen: *I don't think I have.*

He decided to get a second opinion and saw a psychiatrist working at a private hospital who refused to accept payment when he saw Stephen wasn't earning. He interviewed Stephen and went through his medical records. He concluded that the symptoms Stephen was presenting with when admitted to hospital could be attributable to smoking cannabis, and taking imipramine and the sertraline and the amount of stress he was under. (Mania is acknowledged as a potential adverse effect of both imipramine and sertraline.) This psychiatrist did not agree with the diagnosis of manic depression. He also thought it would be appropriate for Stephen to stop taking the sulpiride.

Stephen's usual psychiatrist refused to accept the second opinion or even talk to this psychiatrist. Stephen concluded, at this point, that she would rather be right and for him to be ill than for her to be wrong and him be well.

His usual work was as a lorry driver and, even though his psychiatrist said she thought he would be able to return to work, she insisted that he contact the DVLA (Driving and Vehicle Licensing Authority) to inform them of his 'condition', saying that otherwise, she would. As a result, he lost his HGV (heavy goods vehicle) licence. He was granted a car drivers' licence for one year which was conditional on him complying with treatment. He decided he would rather risk losing this licence than comply with treatment he didn't agree with.

When interviewed, Stephen said he didn't find the sulpiride too bad. It had made him quite tired and a bit emotionally dull, and he put on some weight. He had muscle twitches in, for example, his face, arm, leg and stomach. He also had some neuralgia (nerve pain) in his face and elsewhere. Later he checked the report from his second-opinion psychiatrist and found that he said Stephen had an almost totally absent sex drive, clammy hands, difficulty with speech and noticeable stiffness around the mouth which he attributed to dyskinesia.

Stephen did a lot of reading and felt that if he was going to be on a neuroleptic, sulpiride was the best one. But he also knew about the possible long-term consequences of taking any neuroleptic, such as dopamine supersensitivity and physical health problems, and it was for this reason that he wanted to come off it. Some advantages of sulpiride over other neuroleptics were that it is a low-potency drug which makes it easier to divide into small portions, and it is available in liquid form, which also makes it easier to reduce by small amounts.

Stephen felt supported in his decision to come off by people he spoke to on the Battle Against Tranquillisers (BAT) helpline. Although BAT was set up primarily to help people to come off benzodiazepines, they were knowledgeable about neuroleptics and willing to help. Stephen remembers one particularly useful conversation:

> *I spoke to someone who really seemed to know what they were talking about and was able to give me some moral support and talk things through in a good and logical way.…I was really impressed with the person from BAT saying, 'It's OK not to take these drugs', and it gave me a lot of courage to think, 'I'm not sectioned, I'm stable, I will continue with this.'*

Stephen's partner was also agreeable to him trying to come off the sulpiride.

Stephen thought it best for his psychiatrist to know so that, if he became psychotic, she would be aware that he was on a low dose of sulpiride and not assume he was still on a higher dose and then give him even more. But first he read up on the Mental Health Act to make sure he couldn't be sectioned if she thought he was going to be ill. When he told her, she wasn't happy about it, but couldn't actually stop him.

Stephen did get some encouragement and advice from a third psychiatrist. He wrote to Loren Mosher in the USA, who was well known for his opposition to the routine use of neuroleptics. (Loren Mosher died in 2004.) Stephen was interviewed for the CWCO research in the office where he worked as an advocate and Mosher's reply was printed on to a laminated card and fixed to the wall. He had written:

> *Dear Stephen,*
>
> *Please, as the Grateful Dead would say, 'keep on truckin'. You have lots of support. Never mind that psychiatrists have lost their way. Your way is the way and will work but take time. Remember, if you feel really badly a month or so after the last dose of your drug that is a withdrawal*

symptom(s). Many folks have trouble sleeping at such times and I advise you to use benadryl, an over-the-counter antihistamine, to help you sleep. I have learned that lack of sleep is one of the most difficult things folks endure and restoring it is usually a godsend. Good luck, especially with your advocacy work. People REALLY need advocates like you to face the power and authority of the medical establishment.

Best

Loren Mosher

Stephen also talked to his GP, who had a quite different attitude from his psychiatrist. Stephen remembers him saying:

I don't blame you. You don't want to be on this stuff unless you need to be. You might be well for another 20 years even if you've got manic depression, and if you haven't, you'll be well forever.

Stephen decided to reduce the drug in small amounts and take his time, so that any withdrawal effects would show up and fade away before the next reduction. He was already dividing a 200mg tablet into two. Using a razor blade he could divide the halves by four, which meant each portion was approximately 25mg. So his first reduction was to 100mg in the day and 75mg at night, then to 75mg twice a day, and so on.

He described a typical experience of making a reduction:

I don't notice anything within the first week and sometimes feel better. But within two or three weeks, I definitely feel anxious. My palms might get sweaty. I might think, 'I'm going a bit crazy', or start having rapid thoughts. I've felt hot and cold – unable to control my temperature. I've had nerve pains, almost as if electricity is in my face or head; a very strange feeling as if there's a lot of static electricity. Maybe one of the worst things is losing sleep. I've found taking an antihistamine helps. Sometimes I have vivid dreams and wake up at 3 a.m. still in the dreamlike state. It can feel a bit crazy. So I think about what I need to do. I might get up, drink some water, smoke a few cigarettes and then think, 'I'm not dreaming, I'm in control, I can go back to bed and sleep.'

Stephen worked out a rough reduction plan. He decided he needed at least 10 weeks between reductions: three weeks to get the higher dose of the drug out of his system, six weeks to feel OK, and a week to decide if he was going to get ill again. Proceeding in this way, he got down to 25mg twice a day. This was the smallest dose he could divide his pills into, but he felt it was too big a step to go from 25mg to nothing. He asked his GP if sulpiride was available in a lower dose and was told it was not. He then spoke to a relative who was a pharmacist who showed him how you can turn a pill into a liquid solution. It was only when Stephen told his GP he was going to mix up his own medicine that the GP found out he could prescribe sulpiride in liquid form and agreed to do so.

Stephen took advice from BAT that, when changing to a drug in liquid form, it is best to stabilise on the equivalent amount in solid form before reducing. This was 0.6ml, equivalent to 24mg. Having done that, he proceeded to make small reductions at a time. When interviewed in 2004 he was intending to slowly reduce each dose by 0.05ml at a time.

Stephen finished coming off sulpiride in June 2005 and was discharged from mental health services in September that year. His psychiatrist said he has no more chance of becoming unwell than anyone else. He continued to work full time as an advocate and said, 'I've got my life back.' He still had to submit to medical exams for his car driver's licence but the last one was granted for three years.

COMMENT ON STEPHEN'S STORY

Stephen was extraordinarily resourceful in seeking out information and support. This enabled him to maintain his stance that he wasn't manic depressive, refuse antimanic medication and eventually get off the sulpiride. He had to battle with a psychiatrist, but not with psychiatry. By the time he started systematically tapering the sulpiride he had secured the backing of two psychiatrists and his GP. Ultimately he was proved to be right about the diagnosis and his ability to live without the drugs. But it is not hard to see how a less persistent and confident person could have ended up as a lifelong mental patient.

This detailed account of how Stephen came off the sulpiride has been included as a concrete example of someone acting on the advice given by experts such as Phil Thomas, Rufus May, Peter Breggin and David Cohen (see Appendix 1) to come off very slowly. Stephens's description of the symptoms he experienced whenever he reduced the dose suggests that he might not have succeeded if he had followed more standard advice and tried to come off in under a month. Only 27 per cent of the people taking part in the CWCO survey who tried to come off a neuroleptic took more than six months. Like other people in the survey, Stephen ran into problems when he tried to obtain the drug in a low dose or liquid form and was told by his doctor that it wasn't available. Again, it took resourcefulness on his part to succeed.

The driving licence story is a reminder that it is not just mental health legislation that puts pressure on people to take drugs. Stephen had to be prepared to take the risk of losing not only his HGV licence but also his car driver's licence in refusing antimanic medication.

Faith's Story: Little Scope for Taking Risks

When interviewed, Faith was 54 years old, had been on neuroleptic drugs since she was 23 and was taking trifluoperazine (Stelazine). She had a diagnosis of schizophrenia. Over this time she had tried coming off neuroleptics many times but had not yet succeeded. She was also prescribed the sleeping pill, zopiclone, which she took occasionally.

She didn't like having the diagnosis or taking the drugs, although she thought they had helped her. In many respects her life was going well. At one time she was unemployed, virtually homeless and her daughter was on the 'at risk' register. She had been sectioned under the Mental Health Act. At the time of the interview she had a job and was buying her own flat. She went to the gym regularly, looked after her granddaughter, attended church and also visited a drop-in centre. But these successes can create their own pressures. For example, she was very aware that she was only expected to take a maximum of ten days off sick a year and so felt she couldn't risk becoming unwell.

She looked back at a time when she used to see the same psychiatrist and built up a trusting and supportive relationship with him. Since then she had seen a psychiatrist every three months, but they changed every six months, which she thought was because they were at a teaching hospital. So she only ever saw each psychiatrist twice and they didn't get to know who she was. She thought they found it hard to see past the label:

> *Because they say you suffer from schizophrenia, they say that everything you say is lies. When I had problems with my neighbours and all sort of problems I had nobody to help me. So everywhere I go I always have to have proof that I'm not making up lies because they say that schizophrenic people don't live in the real world, you know. When I got my O-levels after being ill, one of the doctors asked me if somebody had sat the exams for me. You know, they didn't believe that I managed to go back to college and train my mind to pass the exams.*

She also thought they should have offered more help than just drugs:

> *When I became unwell, they didn't find out what is the problem that I have. They just give me drugs. As a black person, they don't give you talking therapy or find out nothing to help you. I had so much problems and nobody tried to help me but they gave me a heap of drugs and I had to cope over the years.*

She spoke of a time when she felt badly treated by a psychiatrist, which she contrasted with his attitude to another patient:

Faith: *I notice he had another patient who was nicely dressed and he would greet her and at the time I was on the dole and didn't have much money to dress up and look nice.*

Interviewer: *So do you think he treated you differently from this other patient?*

Faith: *Yes definitely, because I wasn't being positive. I was way down in the dumps, I wasn't being positive and I suppose he might have felt I was a dead loss.*

She was seeing a counsellor but she found that service for herself, through her workplace – it wasn't offered through mental health services. She had also sought to understand her mental health issues through reading books from a library she worked in and by studying O-level psychology.

She talked about her Christianity:

> *I believe in God and I go to church. When I was a child, in Jamaica, I used to play a lot of truancy and get caned a lot. The only thing that used to help me was going to church with my auntie and my cousin. They would sing hymns and I would feel at peace. I've grown up with that. I left the church but when I became unwell I went back and brought my daughter into the church.*

It was the strength she got from her religion that allowed her to believe she could get off the drugs, and the last time she tried was quite typical in that respect. She was responding to a sermon in which the preacher had said that God can heal, that Jesus used to heal and if you pray and have faith, you can be healed. She felt she could be strong and just believe in God:

> *When I go to church and they say God can heal you, and I'm in that environment, I feel strong enough to do without the drugs. But then I come*

*back home and it's all by myself and there's no support unit around me
and it's not so easy.*

Faith's psychiatrist and GP didn't think she should stop taking her
drugs so she didn't seek to involve them. Her daughter also thought
she should stay on them.

She thought her body has got used to the drugs and so she needed
to come off slowly. She was on one 10mg dose of trifluoperazine a day,
a common amount of this FGN. She decided to start by taking it every
other day. But she found that coming off was affecting her concentration and sleep, as had happened previously, and gave up. She felt she
could have succeeded if she had stayed with it but couldn't afford to
put her job at risk if she needed time off.

She contrasted her situation with someone she sees at the drop-in
who had been able to come off a drug by reducing very slowly but
didn't have a job and the responsibility of looking after a child.

When she was interviewed, Faith had decided she would be better off
staying on her medication. Her doctor was planning to switch her to
an SGN. When contacted again in 2007 she had been on risperidone
(Risperdal) for two years and wasn't sure if was better than the trifluoperazine she had been taking previously. She had not tried coming off
her medication again.

COMMENT ON FAITH'S STORY

Like Brenda and Stephen, Faith comes across as a resourceful person.
She had succeeded in turning her life around, had found some counselling for herself through her workplace and had read up about her
diagnosis. So what was different about Faith's situation that meant she
didn't succeed in coming off her drugs? There were many differences,
but perhaps the key ones were these.

First of all, unlike Brenda, she did experience a withdrawal syndrome.
If she hadn't, having made the decision to try, she could have succeeded
in getting off the drug and then found out how she fared without it.
Some ways her situation differed from Stephen's were that she didn't
have a detailed plan for coming off very slowly and felt less able to live
through the effects of withdrawal. There is a way in which Faith was
trapped by her success, and she compared her situation with that of a
woman she knew who had fewer responsibilities and was able to come
off her drugs.

In the CWCO survey, participants were asked about the role of religion or spirituality in their attempts to come off medication. Table 5.6 shows that two out of five people said they had sought or received help from religion or spirituality and nearly nine out of ten found this to be helpful. For Faith, her Christian beliefs and practice clearly played a positive part in her life, but her belief that God would heal didn't provide her with the practical means to actually stop taking her drugs.

Perhaps, with more support and information, she could have tried and succeeded in coming off over several years.

Faith is explicit about the racism she experienced from some psychiatrists, along with their negative attitudes towards her as someone with a diagnosis of schizophrenia and low social status. But it is difficult to pin down if and how this may have influenced her ability to get off her medication. She had enjoyed a positive relationship with a psychiatrist who, she felt, knew her as a person. Like Brenda and Stephen, her problem wasn't psychiatry as such. But they all experienced some psychiatrists as unable to think about them well, in contrast to others who could.

The Three Stories

These stories challenge simplistic notions summed up by the blanket term, non-compliance. Brenda, Stephen and Faith either went against the advice of their doctors or were prepared to, but none of them could fairly be accused of acting irresponsibly. Brenda was able to convince her psychiatrist to support her, to the credit of both, and she achieved her ambition of getting off lithium. Stephen went against the beliefs of his psychiatrist in refusing antimanic medication and coming off his neuroleptic, but had the agreement of his second-opinion psychiatrist and his GP, and the enthusiastic support of a renowned radical psychiatrist from the USA. In coming off and staying off sulpiride he demonstrated that his beliefs were correct. Faith started to come off her medication slowly, began to experience some adverse effects, decided she wasn't in a good situation to continue and went back on to her usual dose.

Not everyone in the survey exercised such good judgement, as they were willing to admit, but these and other accounts from the survey certainly demonstrate that when it comes to decision making about drugs for people with diagnoses such as schizophrenia and bipolar disorder, doctors don't always get it right, and experimenting with coming off doesn't have to end in disaster.

Doctors and other mental health workers could well look at these three stories and ask themselves what they would do in the situations described. Would they, for example, be prepared to support somebody to exercise their right to try to come off even if, in their judgement, it was the wrong decision? It is worth considering here a quote from the Royal College of Psychiatrists publication, *Fair Deal for Mental Health* (2008, p. 29), which is used in the introduction to this book and proposes that professionals should support people in trying to achieve the goals they set for themselves, even if they believe the goals are not realistic.

The current situation for many people on neuroleptic and antimanic drugs is that they tend to be encouraged, possibly coerced and sometimes compelled to stay on them. Some people are prepared to go against advice and come off anyway, often in secret. If their motivation comes from rebelliousness, anger or impulsiveness or in any way isn't thoroughly thought through, it may be enough to get them to stop. If they don't experience any adverse effects, it might be enough to get them off the drugs for good. But if they do encounter a withdrawal syndrome, they are likely to end up back on them. To equip themselves to come off them against their doctors' wishes and get through a withdrawal syndrome, they need to be able to hunt down information, gather support, have a clear goal and a set of beliefs to support it, and then steer a path of considered risk-taking between cautious passivity and reckless abandon, possibly for a long time. The number of people in a position to achieve all this is obviously going to be a small proportion of those who might benefit from trying with support from professionals or people who have succeeded themselves and have the information and skills to help others.

The suggestion from this research is that it should be possible for doctors, other mental health workers, and their patients to have more harmonious relationships than they sometimes do, when it comes to discussion and decision making about coming off neuroleptics and antimanics. It would require some doctors and other mental health workers to modify their assumptions about the necessity of staying on them. It would require some of them to find a new balance between what they feel is their clinical responsibility and the rights of their patients. It would certainly require many of them to become better informed about best practice in coming off these drugs. But there is enough evidence of good practice from this survey to suggest that it is possible for doctors, other mental health workers and patients to collaborate in constructive and cautious experimentation, to see who can successfully come off their drugs or at least reduce the dose they are on.

7

Key Issues, Suggestions and Conclusion

In this final chapter we revisit the five key issues for the third time, briefly summarising material from Chapters 1 and 2, and adding new thoughts arising from subsequent chapters. Five proposals are made for improving the use of psychiatric drugs and the main messages from this book are brought together in the conclusion.

The Five Key Issues

ADVERSE EFFECTS WHILE TAKING DRUGS

We saw in Chapter 1 that adverse effects of psychiatric drugs are commonly referred to in official literature as side effects and described as unpleasant (see, for example, NICE 2002b, p. 31). They can, however, cause serious damage to people's functioning and health. They can be vast in range, with over 74 possible adverse effects associated with taking England's most prescribed psychiatric drug, the SSRI citalopram (Table 1.1).

The surveys reviewed in Chapter 2 showed that up to 92 per cent of people taking a psychiatric drug reported at least one adverse effect (Rethink 2006, p. 5). Personal accounts capture the impact of adverse effects on people's lives. They also capture the hard choices people sometimes have to make in balancing beneficial and adverse effects. They may be left wondering if they have made the right choice.

The *"All you need to know?"* survey (SAMH 2004) showed instances of people prepared to put up with serious adverse effects if the drugs were helping to relieve symptoms of distress. But participants in the Coping with Coming Off (CWCO) survey cited adverse effects of drugs as the most common reason for wanting to stop taking them (Table 4.6).

In addition to the adverse effects experienced when taking psychiatric drugs there are other effects which people may experience when they stop taking them, which can also be severe and vast in range. For example, according to Joseph Glenmullen (2005, p. 7), over 50 adverse effects of withdrawing from antidepressants have been identified. As with adverse effects when taking drugs, people may experience some or none of them. The CWCO survey suggested that people are more likely to have difficulties coming off drugs the longer they have been taking them (Table 5.8).

Drug companies, regulatory bodies and mental health professionals have been reluctant to acknowledge withdrawal syndromes associated with stopping psychiatric drugs and instead have claimed that these adverse effects are symptoms of distress or illness returning and proof that patients need to stay on the drugs. But it is now generally accepted that people coming off tranquillisers and antidepressants may experience adverse effects (NICE 2007a, p. 22, 2007b, p. 30). Evidence that neuroleptics and antimanics may also cause serious adverse effects on withdrawal has not been so accepted.

CHOICE AND COMPULSION

Psychiatry differs from other branches of medicine in its scope for treating people against their will. The threat of compulsion has cast a shadow over transactions between mental health professionals and service users, causing people who are not being treated under mental health legislation still to feel pressurised into taking psychiatric drugs or powerless about taking them (Table 4.5).

The majority of people prescribed psychiatric drugs are required to give their informed consent, but surveys suggest that a significant proportion of them are not given information about the drugs they are prescribed (Healthcare Commission 2008a, Tables section C). But with drug actions being so complex, and so variable, and with so many potential adverse effects on taking and stopping them, it is questionable how any service user can be sufficiently informed to give informed consent.

Research into service users' experiences has presented us with numerous examples of conflict between service users and professional over decisions about psychiatric drugs and also examples of good practice, with the people involved being able to negotiate and reach agreement.

The CWCO survey showed that people who came off their drugs against their doctor's advice or without informing them were as likely to succeed in coming off them as people who co-operated with their doctor (Table 5.9). This finding challenges assumptions about the irrationality of service users and the ability of doctors to predict who can safely stop taking their drugs.

The NICE clinical guideline, *Medicines Adherence: Involving patients in decisions about prescribed medicines and supporting adherence* (2009a), challenges professionals to engage with service users' doubts about medication and recognise their right to refuse to take drugs. It encourages the good practice that has been identified in the CWCO research and holds out hope for a more collaborative approach.

PEOPLE FROM BLACK AND MINORITY ETHNIC COMMUNITIES

There is a consensus that people from BME communities in the UK are poorly treated by mental health services. This doesn't mean that every minority ethnic group is treated in the same way but overall, they fare less well in mental health services than the white majority. In the *Count Me In: Service User Survey* (MHAC 2005) people from BME communities rated their experiences of inpatient services less favourably than the other people questioned.

The CWCO research showed people from BME communities having significantly different experiences of medication than the other participants. They were more likely to have taken neuroleptics or antimanics, to have experienced drugs as mainly harmful (Table 4.4), to have been compelled to take them (Table 4.5) and to have come off their drugs against their doctor's advice or without telling their doctor (Table 4.7). Yet they were at least as likely to succeed in coming off them as non-BME participants (Table 5.7).

It is difficult to identify specific reasons to account for these different experiences, but the acknowledgement of institutional racism in mental health services in the report commissioned by the Department of Health, *Inside Outside: Improving Mental Health Services for Black and Minority Ethnic Communities in England* (NIMHE 2003, pp. 7, 24), provides a starting point and a framework for understanding and rising to this challenge.

THE RISE AND POSSIBLE FALL OF SSRIS

In Chapter 1 SSRIs were shown to owe their place as the most prescribed drugs in psychiatry more to marketing than evidence of effectiveness. But their dominance as a treatment for mild depression and other conditions was being challenged by guidelines from NICE recommending psychological therapies (for example, NICE 2007b). These were being implemented in England through the Improving Access to Psychological Therapies programme (NIMHE 2007).

The role of SSRIs was challenged further by a meta-analysis which suggested there was little reason to prescribe SSRIs except for the most severely depressed patients or if other treatments were ineffective (Kirsch et al. 2008).

According to the NICE guideline on depression (2007b, p. 24), 'SSRIs are as effective as other types of antidepressants and they usually have less side effects.'

But participants in the *"All you need to know?"* survey (SAMH 2004) rated SSRIs as less helpful for symptom relief (p. 49) than the older tricyclic antidepressants, and they were more likely to experience adverse effects while taking them and when stopping them than people who took tricyclics (p. 50). Overall SSRIs were rated the least helpful of all psychiatric drugs apart from depot neuroleptics (p. 90), and participants in this survey and CWCO were more likely to have difficulties coming off SSRIs than other drugs (Tables A2.2: 5.2).

The SSRI story has been used here to highlight how practitioners and patients can become convinced that newer, patented and more expensive drugs are better than older drugs when the supporting evidence isn't there. Much the same has happened with Z-drugs and SGNs. Like SSRIs, the newer neuroleptics offer more choice and some people prefer them, but claims that they represent a breakthrough in treatment have been shown to be exaggerated.

EFFECTIVENESS

Psychiatric drugs are widely prescribed throughout the Western industrialised world and elsewhere. NICE guidelines recommend them for people diagnosed with depression, generalised anxiety disorder, schizophrenia, bipolar disorder and other similar conditions, although psychological therapies are preferred in some instances.

Yet it is difficult to prove that these drugs are more effective than placebos, especially with the limitations of randomised controlled trials. There is some evidence that although they may provide symptom relief in the short term, long-term outcomes for people taking psychiatric drugs are unimpressive. Any benefits have to be weighed against adverse effects when taking and stopping them.

Surveys of service users demonstrate that people vary a great deal in their responses to psychiatric drugs, making it difficult to predict how any individual will benefit or be harmed by them. Many service users are unsure whether they are benefiting overall from the drugs they take. The *"All you need to know?"* survey (SAMH 2004) found that 28 per cent of people taking psychiatric drugs could be classed as 'satisfied customers', rating them as 'very helpful' (Table 2.2). Participants in this survey rated different drugs of the same type quite variably, emphasising the value of experimenting with different drugs if people are not satisfied with the ones they are on.

Withdrawal syndromes confuse the picture, especially if they are not acknowledged and understood. Adverse effects on stopping drugs can be confused with signs of relapse. The drugs are then erroneously considered to have been keeping the person well, giving a falsely positive impression of their effectiveness.

Suggestions for Improving the Use of Psychiatric Drugs

These six suggestions have been chosen to reflect the themes which have emerged from the material presented in this book. They are intended to show how the use of psychiatric drugs can be improved, with an emphasis on not prescribing them without justification and helping people who don't need to be on psychiatric drugs to successfully withdraw from them.

SERVICE USER-LED INFORMATION AND SUPPORT PROJECTS

Service user-led information and support projects could help people to make informed choices; provide support if they want to think about changing, reducing or coming off their medication and assist them through the withdrawal process if they decide to do it. They should be run, as far as possible, by 'experts by experience' – people who have taken psychiatric drugs themselves.

They could also provide advocacy or link with existing advocacy projects to support people in their negotiations with mental health workers. User-run advocacy projects provide a model, with their ethos of supporting people to think and act for themselves.

Meetings with visiting expert speakers could inform people of the debates about psychiatric drugs. Discussion groups could enable them to share their thoughts and experiences. People who are being compelled to take medication need not be excluded. They still have the right to information and to negotiate with doctors. The projects could also help people make advance decisions.

They are not a new idea; there have been projects offering some of these services for years. One example is the Shropshire Thinking About Medication Group. A series of meetings were set up to help people think about coming off psychiatric drugs. They provided opportunities to access information, exchange views, experiences and support, and listen to and question visiting speakers. In writing about this initiative the facilitators, Guy Holmes, a psychologist, and Marese Hudson, a service user, addressed a key concern that mental health professionals may have about this sort of activity (Holmes & Hudson 2006, p. 10):

> Before the group was set up some anxieties were expressed that the group might be 'anti-medication' or lead to people abruptly stopping their medication and rejecting psychiatric staff and their advice. In fact the opposite seemed to happen, with members taking much more care about taking, reducing or coming off their medication, and entering into more collaborative relationships with their prescribers rather than having disagreements that occasionally led to what was perceived by participants as reckless stopping of medication through anger and frustration with being told they had to take drugs they were very ambivalent about.

The difference between these proposed projects and those with a more specific focus would be in scale and scope. They should be available in every area and receive sufficient and secure funding to enable them to offer the range of services and activities outlined here. Ideally they would be centrally funded with a national office to provide organisational back-up.

A PROGRAMME TO SUPPORT PEOPLE TO GET OFF PSYCHIATRIC DRUGS THEY ARE TAKING UNNECESSARILY

This proposal isn't about the more controversial or less clear arguments about who should stop taking psychiatric drugs or about individuals' decisions. It is about helping the large numbers of people on drugs which, according to guidelines, they shouldn't be taking.

Three UK instances have been highlighted in this book. In Chapter 1 there is reference to the survey commissioned by the TV programme, *Panorama* (2001), whose research estimated that 1.5 million people had taken tranquillisers for more than four months. There is no evidence of this figure having fallen since.

Also in Chapter 1 mention is made of an inquiry by the All Party Parliamentary Group on Dementia, which estimated that 105,000 people with dementia were being prescribed neuroleptics inappropriately (BBC News 2008a).

Finally, Chapter 3 includes a brief description of a project for helping people who had recovered from depression get off SSRIs (Quayle et al. 2008). Extrapolating from the number of people it helped produced a rough estimate of nearly 300,000 people taking SSRIs unnecessarily. This figure does not include people who have been prescribed antidepressants for mild depression and who should be offered psychological therapies instead.

These figures combine to give a total of over 1.9 million people in the UK taking psychiatric drugs but not benefiting from them and possibly experiencing adverse effects. That is more than the combined populations of Belfast, Cardiff, Glasgow, Leicester, Newcastle-upon-Tyne and Oxford, or enough people to fill Wembley Stadium 21 times.

There is no mystery about how to help these people successfully withdraw from their drugs. Many people who have been prescribed tranquillisers for too long will still be able to stop them easily after a discussion with their doctor or another mental health professional.

Professor Heather Ashton, an expert on withdrawal from tranquillisers, presented her ideas for the support that should be made available to people who have difficulties withdrawing from them to the All-Party Action Group on Tranquilliser Addiction, at the House of Commons. This is a summary (based on Ashton 2006):

- Dedicated NHS benzodiazepine withdrawal clinics staffed by trained doctors and health-care workers.
- Involvement of health-care workers in GP surgeries. These could include community nurses and pharmacists, counsellors and psychological therapists to work with GPs, suggesting and supervising withdrawal schedules and providing frequent and long-term support for patients.
- Provision of many more psychological therapists to whom patients have prompt access. Ashton suggests that less formal therapies than cognitive behavioural therapy are applicable to benzodiazepine patients and fully trained psychologists are rarely necessary, though specific training in benzodiazepine problems is important.

- Financial support for self-help groups. These groups can be extremely helpful and are sometimes run by ex-benzodiazepine users who understand the problems.

Research by Professor Clive Ballard and colleagues (Ballard et al. 2008) described in Chapter 3 suggests that people diagnosed with dementia can stop taking their low doses of neuroleptics without experiencing withdrawal syndromes.

The Shropshire project demonstrated how GPs' patients can successfully be encouraged and supported by a Community Psychiatric Nurse to withdraw from SSRIs.

There are some people, especially those who have taken tranquillisers for decades, who believe so strongly that they couldn't cope without their drugs that, on balance, the nocebo effect from the fear of stopping them may outweigh the potential benefits. There are others who will need to use a residential facility to break their dependence. But most of these 1.9 million people will be able to get off their drugs if they are given information, encouragement and support. What is required is the political will to prioritise and organise it. This begins with acknowledging the problem.

ALL PSYCHIATRIC DRUGS SHOULD BE PRODUCED IN LOW DOSES TO AID TAPERING

This is a simple proposal for helping people withdraw from psychiatric drugs safely. Some are not available in sufficiently low doses. People then have to resort to cutting them with razor blades, opening up capsules, missing alternate doses and switching to other drugs, each of which can create problems and discourage people from following slow tapering regimes.

Regulatory bodies should require manufacturers of psychiatric drugs to produce them in suitably low doses or, preferably, in liquid form.

STRENGTHENING REGULATION

The SSRI story has shown how little progress has been made in regulation since the similar sequence of events that eventually led to tight restrictions on the use of tranquillisers.

Criticisms of the UK's Medicines and Health products Regulatory Agency (MHRA) apply equally or more so to the USA's Food and Drug

Administration (FDA), which lagged behind the MHRA in issuing warnings about SSRIs (Glenmullen 2005, pp. vii–xi). Objective evaluation of drugs is further undermined in the USA, and also New Zealand, by direct-to-consumer advertising which creates demand from patients for particular branded medicines.

In the UK the House of Commons Health Committee (2005, pp. 114–20) made a series of recommendations for strengthening regulation in its report *The Influence of the Pharmaceutical Industry*. They were intended to shift the balance of power from manufacturers to patients with stronger, more proactive and wider-ranging powers for regulatory bodies. In particular it called for an independent review of the MHRA. It proposed that the review should be governed by principles which included the need for greater independence from government, greater independence from the pharmaceutical industry and inclusion of the public in policy-making and implementation.

In a proposal intended to distance organisations which should be protecting the public from the undue influence of drug companies, it recommended that responsibility for representing the interests of the pharmaceutical industry should move from the Department of Health to the Department of Trade and Industry (now the Department for Business, Enterprise and Regulatory Reform).

Strengthening regulation along these lines would encourage a more cautious use of medicines, including psychiatric drugs, and help to avoid repetition of serious errors of the past.

MORE RESEARCH INTO SERVICE USERS' EXPERIENCES OF PSYCHIATRIC DRUGS

Most research into psychiatric drugs is funded by companies seeking licences and recognition for their products. As discussed in Chapter 1, their clinical trials focus on short-term symptom relief, using questionable methodology. There is an outstanding need for studies of outcome and treatments over decades rather than months, as Trevor Howard Turner pointed out in his *BMJ* editorial (2004, p. 1059).

Research into the experiences of service users has been patchy. The surveys reviewed in Chapter 2 have produced some valuable information, but this research is rarely repeated so that results can be validated. The Healthcare Commission *Survey of Users of Mental Health Services* (2008a) is exceptional because it is on such a large scale and repeated annually so that progress towards targets can be measured. What it doesn't do and isn't intended to do is explore people's experiences and thoughts about being users of mental health services; what they are offered and what they might prefer instead. The surveys which do this are conducted by voluntary organisations which occasionally obtain funding for one-off projects. In an era in which the views and wants of service users are being taken more seriously, there is a compelling case for funding more research that taps into their thoughts and experiences.

The following proposals are for research which would build on the themes that emerge from the exploration of service users' experiences and views presented here:

* Repetition of the *Count Me In: The National Mental Health and Ethnicity Census 2005 Service User Survey* (MHAC 2005) every five years. This would help to establish whether service providers are succeeding in bringing the level of satisfaction of inpatients from BME communities up to that of non-BME inpatients.
* The *"All you need to know?"* survey (SAMH 2004) produced a wealth of information. In particular it offered a reality check on the newer medications, SSRIs and SGNs, which were not as highly rated, relative to older drugs, as might have been expected. It would be informative to repeat it in other countries or states to find out if these findings are replicated.
* There has been some continuity in the series of surveys conducted by Mind from the *That's Life! Survey on tranquillisers* (Lacey & Woodward 1985) to CWCO. A useful next step would be to focus specifically on the experiences of people who have taken neuroleptics. The finding that people who were non-compliant were as likely to succeed in coming off them as those who did so with the involvement of their doctor has important implications for the practice of prescribing neuroleptics long term and devoting considerable resources and attention to trying to ensure people take them, but it needs to be followed up with a larger sample. A detailed survey of people who have stayed on or come off neuroleptics could contribute a great deal to a much needed debate.

Surveys of service users offer value for money. Those discussed in Chapter 2 have each made a significant difference to our understanding of the benefits and problems associated with taking psychiatric drugs. It is time for such surveys to become commonplace rather than occasional events.

A REVIEW OF THE ROUTINE LONG-TERM USE OF NEUROLEPTICS

In addition to the CWCO survey, throughout this book there are references to reviews and studies that raise questions about the routine long-term use of neuroleptics with people diagnosed with schizophrenia and similar disorders.

We saw in Chapter 1 that Trevor Howard Turner (2004, p. 1058) has raised doubts about whether they improve long-term outcomes, that Robert Whitaker (2004) has reviewed the research into neuroleptics and concluded that the practice of maintaining schizophrenic patients on these drugs is not supported by evidence and that Joanna Moncrieff has proposed that neuroleptics do not have a specific antipsychotic action and any benefit comes from their sedating effect (2007).

In Chapter 3 we saw that David Cohen (1997, pp. 197–8) criticised studies that purport to show high rates of relapse in people who have their neuroleptic medication replaced with a placebo. He suggested, instead, that these studies demonstrate that there is a withdrawal syndrome associated with coming off these drugs. When people come off them slowly they are less likely to relapse, suggesting the possibility of more people successfully living without them.

Current trends, such as the promotion of shared decision-making and adherence (Chapter 1) and the recovery approach (Introduction), suggest a more flexible approach to prescribing these drugs but, meanwhile, the practice of prescribing them long term carries on and the focus of mental health services tends to be on ensuring people keep taking them. It is time to put this psychiatric practice under scrutiny with an independent public inquiry that features a high degree of input from people who have taken these drugs.

Conclusion

In the Introduction several trends in mental health services in the UK that suggested a more collaborative approach towards making decisions about medication were described. The Care Programme Approach, shared decision-making and adherence in prescribing, the

New Ways of Working initiative and the recovery approach all have implications for more negotiation between professionals and patients or service users.

Chapter 1 introduced evidence and arguments that questioned assumptions about the effectiveness of psychiatric drugs. Testimony from service users in Chapter 2 emphasised how differently people respond to drugs and the dilemmas of taking drugs that might be beneficial in some ways but harmful in others. Chapter 3 highlighted the difficulties of deciding how long people should stay on drugs and the withdrawal syndromes associated with coming off them. The chapters based on CWCO emphasised the conflicts that occur between mental health workers and service users about stopping medication and gave examples of them being resolved.

These themes suggest a new approach to prescribing which is consistent with the approach to treatment proposed in a joint position paper on recovery produced by three key UK organisations, the Care Services Improvement Partnership (CSIP), the Royal College of Psychiatrists and the Social Care Institute for Excellence (SCIE). *A common purpose: Recovery in future mental health services* (SCIE 2007, p. 6) had this to say about the role of treatment in recovery:

> It remains important that treatment decisions are guided by evidence, but given the high rates of discontinuation of treatment, how such decisions are made may be as important as the decision itself. People in recovery speak clearly about the value of negotiation and collaboration concerning treatment decisions and the evidence of an individual's experience, of whether something works or not in practice, given priority over general beliefs about what should work. Treatment is thus recontextualised as one out of many tools that can support recovery.

It seems that professional opinion and the desires of service users are drawing closer. There is real hope that a more flexible attitude to medication from mental health workers will offer service users the choices they desire. And if it is possible to sum up this new approach in a sentence it is perhaps this:

Decision making about whether to prescribe psychiatric drugs and about changing, reducing and stopping medication should be made in a spirit of cautious experimentation, open-mindedness and collaboration, with the service user or patient being respected as the person whose wishes are ultimately paramount.

Critical Reflection Box 7.1

Final Thoughts

Exercise A is for people who responded to the questions in Critical Reflection Box I.1 and have read through this book.

Exercise B is for anyone who has read this chapter.

A

This is a time to reflect on how your views about psychiatric drugs have been confirmed or challenged by what you have read.

Would you now change your mind about your answers to questions 1–5 and 7? If so, what did you read that affected your views?

B

1. What are the challenges to professionals of the proposed new approach to prescribing described in the conclusion?
2. What are the challenges to you in your professional practice or personally?
3. Do you agree or disagree with this approach and why?

Appendix 1
Sources of Practical Information about Coming off Psychiatric Drugs

Publications

Advice on Medication (booklet), Phil Thomas and Rufus May, Hearing Voices Network, 2003.

Coming Off Antidepressants: How to use – and stop using – antidepressants safely, Joseph Glenmullen, Robinson, 2006. (Written for the UK.)

'Coming off medication?', Guy Holmes and Marese Hudson. Originally appeared in *OpenMind* 23, September/October 2003. Can be read at http://www.mind.org.uk/Shopping/Openmind/Extracts/Extract+from+Issue+123+Coming+off+medication.htm

Coming off Psychiatric Drugs: Successful withdrawal from neuroleptics, antidepressants, lithium, carbamazepine and tranquilizers, ed. Peter Lehmann, Peter Lehmann Publishing, 2004.

Harm Reduction Guide to Coming Off Psychiatric Drugs, Icarus Project and Freedom Center, USA, 2007. Can be accessed at http://freedom-center.org/node/318

Healing Schizophrenia: Using medication wisely, John Watkins, Michelle Anderson Publishing, 2006.

Making Sense of Coming Off Psychiatric Drugs (booklet), Katherine Darton, Mind, 2005. Can be read at http://www.mind.org.uk/Information/Booklets/Making+sense/Making+sense+of+coming+off+psychiatric+drugs.htm

Psychiatric Drugs Explained, 5th edn, David Healy, Elsevier Churchill Livingstone, 2008.

The Antidepressant Solution, Joseph Glenmullen, Free Press, 2006. (Written for the USA.)

Your Drug May be Your Problem: How and why to stop taking psychiatric medications, Peter Breggin & David Cohen, Da Capo Press, 2007.

Websites

Benzodiazepine addiction, withdrawal and recovery: http://www.
benzo.org.uk/

Coming off psychiatric medication: http://www.comingoff.com

Email discussion list for people interested in withdrawal from psychiatric drugs: http://lists.topica.com/lists/coming-off

Mind's website includes an article 'Halting SSRIs' by David Healy:
http://www.mind.org.uk/NR/rdonlyres/59D68F19-F69C-4613-
BD40-A0D8B38D1410/0/DavidHealyHaltingSSRIs.pdf

Seroxat and SSRI User Group: http://www.seroxatusergroup.org.uk

Organisations

BATTLE AGAINST TRANQUILLISERS

PO Box 65B
Bristol
BS99 1XP

Telephone 0117 966 3629 or 965 3463

Website http://www.bataid.org

MEDICINES AND HEALTHCARE PRODUCTS REGULATORY AGENCY (MHRA)

Report adverse effects, including withdrawal effects, of any medication (including over-the-counter and herbal remedies) to the agency via the website, www.yellowcard.gov.uk, on the Yellow Card hotline freephone 0808 100 3352 or on cards obtainable from your GP or local pharmacy.

MIND

Mind has an information service which can be accessed by phone, email or post.

Mind
PO Box 277
Manchester
M60 3XN
Mind*info*Line 0845 766 0163

Instant interpreting and translation service in 170 languages.

Deaf or speech-impaired enquirers can use the same phone number (if using BT Textdirect add the prefix 18001).

Email info@mind.org.uk

Appendix 2

Adverse Effects when Coming off Psychiatric Drugs

This appendix includes figures from the survey by the Scottish Association for Mental Health, *"All you need to know?"* (SAMH 2004), as well as the Coping with Coming Off (CWCO) survey. There is more information about *"All you need to know?"* in Chapter 2.

More people participated in the SAMH survey than the CWCO survey and so it is possible, using data from that survey, to show what proportion of people coming off specific drugs experienced unwanted effects. All drugs (or drug groups) where the sample was 20 or more have been included. (*"All you need to know?"* used slightly different categories than CWCO and some figures have been moved around so that the categories here are the same as those used in CWCO and throughout this book.)

For the CWCO survey we chose a sample of people where about half had succeeded in coming off their drug(s). This intentional bias may then have affected the proportion who said they experienced difficulties when they tried coming off their drug(s).

"All you need to know?" only included drugs that had been newly prescribed in the previous three years. This means that the experiences of people on drugs for a long time were not strongly represented. The CWCO data in Table A2.1 show that when people had been on drugs for longer than a year they were much more likely to experience difficulties when trying to come off them.

Table A2.1 People experiencing difficulties coming off/how long on drug (%)*

Less than a year	37
One to five years	76
More than five years	68
All	63

*People coming off a single drug.

Source: CWCO survey.

The percentages of people in *"All you need to know?"* that experienced unwanted effects when trying to come off their drugs was, then, likely to be lower than it would have been if it had included more people who had been on their drugs for longer. These influences on the different surveys go some way towards explaining the difference between the figures: in the CWCO survey, 63 per cent said they experienced difficulties when coming off their drugs(s) (Table A2.1) and in *"All you need to know?"* the percentage of people who said they experienced unwanted effects when coming off was 42 per cent (table A2.2). Arguably, 'experienced difficulties', used in the CWCO survey, is less specific than 'experienced unwanted effects', used in *"All you need to know?"*, and this may also have contributed to the CWCO figure being higher.

Table A2.2 shows that SSRIs were the drugs most associated with unwanted effects on withdrawing. With SGNs in second place, this table is headed by the two most recently introduced categories of drug, heralded as improvements on previous antidepressants and neuroleptics.

The rest of the tables in this appendix show the percentages of people experiencing unwanted effects when coming off specific drugs. Also included are the half-lives of the drugs. Table A2.3 shows that the antidepressants with shorter half-lives tend to cause more problems when people try to come off them, though there are exceptions. Table A2.4 doesn't demonstrate any link between half-lives of neuroleptics and unwanted effects when coming off them.

Table A2.2 People experiencing unwanted effects when coming off different types of psychiatric drugs (%)

	No.	%
SSRI antidepressants	351	50
SGNs	190	44
Antimanics	102	38
Other antidepressants	53	38
FGNs	160	37
Tranquillisers	64	36
Tricyclic and related antidepressants	99	33
*All drugs**	*1037*	*42*

* The figures for 'All drugs' include the eight people who tried coming off a depot neuroleptic.

Source: Data taken from SAMH 2004.

Table A2.3 People experiencing unwanted effects when coming off antidepressants (%)

Drug	Type	No.	%	Half-life
Paroxetine	SSRI	96	57	24 hrs
Venlafaxine	SSRI	83	57	5 hrs
Sertraline	SSRI	37	49	26 hrs
Citalopram	SSRI	54	43	1.5 days
Fluoxetine	SSRI	78	37	4–6 days
Trazodone	Tricyclic related	22	36	Not available
Mirtazapine	Other	25	28	20–40 hrs
Lofepramine	Tricyclic	22	23	5 hrs

Source: Data taken from SAMH 2004 and Darton 2005.

Table A2.4 People experiencing unwanted effects when coming off neuroleptics (%)

Drug	Type	No.	%	Half-life
Risperidone	SGN*	42	55	24 hrs
Clozapine	SGN	26	46	12 hrs
Haloperidol	FGN	21	43	20 hrs
Quetiapine	SGN	27	41	7 hrs
Olanzapine	SGN	74	39	3 days
Amisulpride	SGN	20	35	24 hrs
Chlorpromazine	FGN	67	30	20–40 hrs

* FGN = first-generation neuroleptic; SGN = second-generation neuroleptic.

Source: Data taken from SAMH 2004 and Darton 2005.

Table A2.5 People experiencing unwanted effects when coming off antimanics (%)

Drug	No.	%	Half-life
Lithium	50	46	1 day
Carbamazepine	20	35	16–24 hrs
Valproate	23	17	14 hrs

Source: Data taken from SAMH 2004 and Darton 2005.

The numbers of people who had tried coming off specific tranquillisers were not sufficient to produce a table, but a big difference can be seen between people's experiences of trying to come off tranquillisers used as sleeping pills (hypnotics) and those used for anxiety (anxiolytics). Of the 19 people who tried coming off a hypnotic, 63 per cent experienced unwanted effects but, in contrast, for the 45 people coming off anxiolytics, the figure was only 24 per cent. Anxiolytics tend to have longer half-lives than hypnotics.

References

Allen, C. 2007, 'Form of torment'. Retrieved 3 July 2007 from http://society.guardian.co.uk/itsmylife/story/0,,2064574,00.html

American Psychiatric Association 2000, *Diagnostic and Statistical Manual of Mental Disorders, Fourth Edition, Text Revision: DSM-IV-TR*, American Psychiatric Association, Arlington, Virginia.

Appleby, L. 2007, *Breaking Down Barriers: Clinical cases for change*, Department of Health, London.

Ashton, H. 2006, 'Benzodiazepines: Problems and ? solutions'. Retrieved 14 December 2007 from http://www.benzo.org.uk/

Ballard, C., Hanney, M. L., Theodoulou, M., Douglas, S., McShane, R., Kossakowski, K., Gill, R., Juszczak, E., Yu, L.-M. & Jacoby, R. 2009, 'The dementia antipsychotic withdrawal trail (DART-AD): Long-term follow-up of a randomised placebo-controlled trail', *The Lancet Neurology*, February, 8(21), pp. 151–7.

Ballard, C., Margallo Lana, M., Theodoulou, M., Douglas, S., McShane, R., Jacoby, R., Kossakowski, K., Yu, L.-M. & Juszczak, E. 2008, 'A Randomised, Blinded, Placebo-Controlled Trial in Dementia Patients Continuing or Stopping Neuroleptics (The DART-AD Trial)', *PLoS Medicine*. Retrieved 27 May 2008 from http://medicine.plosjournals.org/perlserv/?request=get-document&doi=10.1371/journal.pmed.0050076

Barondes, S.H. 2005, *Better than Prozac*, Oxford University Press, Oxford.

BBC News 2005. 'Sedatives risk fears for elderly'. Retrieved 22 August 2008 from http://news.bbc.co.uk/1/hi/health/4424678.stm

BBC News 2008a, 'MPs urge cut in dementia drug use'. Retrieved 16 July 2008 from http://newsvote.bbc.co.uk/mpapps/pagetools/print/news.bbc.co.uk/1/hi/health/7366416.stm

BBC News 2008b, 'Doctors "ignoring drugs warning"'. Retrieved 22 August 2008 from http://news.bbc.co.uk/1/hi/programmes/file_on_4/7457132.stm

BBC News 2008c, 'Talking therapy plans under fire'. Retrieved 23 August 2008 from http://news.bbc.co.uk/1/hi/health/7486132.stm

Bennett, J. 2008, 'Supporting Recovery: Medication Management in Mental Health Care', in J. E. Lynch & S. Trenoweth (eds), *Contemporary issues in Mental Health Nursing*, John Wiley, Chichester, pp. 117–31.

Bhui, K. & Bhugra, D. 1999, 'Pharmacotherapy across ethnic and cultural boundaries', *Mental Health Practice*, June, 2(9), pp. 10–14.

Bhui, K. & Olajide, D. 1999, 'Psychiatry and Cultural Relativity', in K. Bhui & D. Olajide (eds), *Mental Health Service Provision for a Multi-cultural Society*, W. B. Saunders, London, pp. 69–82.

Black Mental Health UK 2007, 'Royal Assent of 2007 Mental Health Act comes with "health warning" to black communities.' Press release. Retrieved 4 August 2007 from http://www.blackmentalhealth.org.uk/main/index.php?option=com_content&task=view&id=47&Itemid=46

Black service user group 2000, recording of discussion on good practice in medicine.

Bracken, P. & Thomas, P. 2005, *Postpsychiatry: Mental health in a postmodern world*, Oxford University Press, Oxford.

Breggin, P. 2006, 'Intoxication anosognosia: The spellbinding effect of psychiatric drugs', *Ethical Human Psychology and Psychiatry*, 8(3), pp. 201–16.

Breggin, P. & Cohen, D. 1999, *Your Drug May Be Your Problem: How and why to stop taking psychiatric medications*, Perseus Books, Reading, MA.

Brennan, C. 2000, 'St John's wort – a natural remedy for depression?' Retrieved 5 September 2008 from http://www.netdoctor.co.uk/special_reports/depression/stjwort.htm

British Psychological Society 2000, *Recent advances in understanding mental illness and psychotic experiences*, British Psychological Society, Leicester.

Brook, R. 2004, 'Mind's Chief Executive resigns from expert panel over lack of openness in UK drug regulation'. Press release. Retrieved 5 October 2007 from http://www.mind.org.uk/News+policy+and+campaigns/Press+archive/mhraresigning.htm

Campbell, P. 2005, 'From Little Acorns – The mental health service user movement', in *Beyond the Water Towers: The unfinished revolution in mental health services 1985–2005*, Sainsbury Centre for Mental Health, London. Retrieved 11 August 2008 from http://www.scmh.org.uk/publications/beyond_the_water_towers.aspx?ID=411

Campbell, P., Cobb, A., & Darton, K. 1998, *Psychiatric Drugs: Users' experiences and current policy and practice*, Mind, London.

Carson, R. 1997, 'Costly Compromises: A Critique of the Diagnostic and Statistical Manual of Mental Disorders', in S. Fisher and R. Greenberg (eds), *From Placebo to Panacea: Putting psychiatric drugs to the test*, John Wiley, Hoboken, NJ, pp. 98–112.

Carter, S., Taylor, D. & Levenson, R. 2005, *A question of choice – compliance in medicine taking*, 3rd edn, Medicines Partnership, Keele. Retrieved 31 July 2007 from http://www.npc.co.uk/med_partnership/resource/major-reviews/a-question-of-choice.html

Chamberlain, J. 1988, *On Our Own*, Mind, London.

Churchill, R., Owen, G., Singh, S. & Hotopf, M. 2007, *International experiences of using community treatment orders*, Department of Health, London. Retrieved 15 July 2007 from http://www.dh.gov.uk/en/Publicationsandstatistics/Publications/PublicationsPolicyAndGuidance/DH_072730

Cobb, A., Darton, K. & Juttla, K. 2001, *Mind's Yellow Card for Reporting Drug Side Effects: A report of users' experiences*, Mind, London.

Cohen, D. 1997, 'A Critique of the Use of Neuroleptic Drugs', in S. Fisher & R. P. Greenberg (eds) *From Placebo to Panacea: Putting psychiatric drugs to the test*, John Wiley, Hoboken, NJ, pp. 173–228.

Darton, K. 2005, *Making Sense of Coming Off Psychiatric Drugs*, Mind, London.

Department of Health 1999, *National Service Framework for Mental Health*, Department of Health, London.

Department of Health 2001a, *The Mental Health Policy Implementation Guide*, Department of Health, London. Retrieved 10 August 2008 from http://www.dh.gov.uk/en/Publicationsandstatistics/Publications/PublicationsPolicyAndGuidance/DH_4009350

Department of Health 2001b, *Prescription Cost Analysis England 2000*, Department of Health, London. Retrieved 25 November 2008 from http://www.dh.gov.uk/en/Publicationsandstatistics/Publications/PublicationsStatistics/DH_4005260

Department of Health 2002, *Prescription Cost Analysis England 2001*, Department of Health, London. Retrieved 25 November 2008 from http://www.dh.gov.uk/en/Publicationsandstatistics/Publications/PublicationsStatistics/DH_4008448

Department of Health 2005, *Delivering race equality in mental health care*, Department of Health, London. Retrieved 4 August 2007 from http://www.dh.gov.uk/en/Publicationsandstatistics/Publications/PublicationsPolicyAndGuidance/DH_4100773

Department of Health 2006a, *Medicines Matter*, Department of Health, London. Retrieved 19 August 2008 from http://www.dh.gov.uk/en/Publicationsandstatistics/Publications/PublicationsPolicyAndGuidance/DH_064325

Department of Health 2006b, *From values to action: The Chief Nursing Officer's review of mental health nursing*, Department of Health, London. Retrieved 20 August 2008 from http://www.dh.gov.uk/en/Publicationsandstatistics/Publications/PublicationsPolicyAndGuidance/DH_4133839

Department of Health 2007, *Mental Health: New Ways of Working for Everyone*, Department of Health, London. Retrieved 20 August 2008 from http://www.dh.gov.uk/en/AdvanceSearchResult/index.htm?searchTerms=Mental+Health%3A+new+Ways+of+Working+for+Everyone%27

Department of Health 2008, *Refocusing the care programme approach: Policy and positive practice guidance*, Department of Health, London. Retrieved 1 September 2008 from http://www.dh.gov.uk/en/Publicationsandstatistics/Publications/PublicationsPolicyAndGuidance/DH_083647

Dilner, L. 2004, 'Why millions of women are hooked on happy pills', *Observer*, 21 April. Retrieved 7 August 2007 from http://www.guardian.co.uk/gender/story/0,,1194466,00.html

Dobson, R. 2007, 'Huge weight gain reported by patients on prescription drugs', *Independent*, 24 June. Retrieved 25 December 2007 from http://news.independent.co.uk/health/article2701322.ece

DrugScope 2008, 'Benzodiazepines'. Retrieved 23 August 2008 from http://www.drugscope.org.uk/resources/drugsearch/drugsearchpages/benzodiazepines.htm

Ethical Corporation 2004, 'Spitzer's drug test'. Retrieved 1 October 2008 from http://www.ethicalcorp.com/content.asp?ContentID=2759

Ferguson, B. 2005, 'A recommended benzodiazepine withdrawal programme', *Prescriber*, 19 September, pp. 20–6.

Fisher, S. & Greenberg, R. P. 1997, *From Placebo to Panacea: Putting psychiatric drugs to the test*, John Wiley, Hoboken, NJ.

Glenmullen, J. 2001, *Prozac Backlash: Overcoming the dangers of Prozac, Zoloft, Paxil and other antidepressants with safe, effective alternatives*, Touchstone, New York.

Glenmullen, J. 2005, *The Antidepressant Solution: A step-by-step guide to safely overcoming antidepressant withdrawal, dependence, and 'addiction'*, Free Press, New York.

Harrow, M. & Jobe, T. H. 2007, 'Factors Involved in Outcome and Recovery in Schizophrenia Patients Not on Antipsychotic Medications: A 15-Year Multifollow-Up Study', *Journal of Mental and Nervous Disease*, 195, 5 May, pp. 406–14.

Healthcare Commission 2004, *Survey of Users of Mental Health Services 2004*, Commission for Healthcare Audit and Inspection, London. Retrieved 2 October 2008 from http://www.healthcarecommission.org.uk/healthcareproviders/nationalfindings/surveys/healthcareproviders/surveysofpatients/mentalhealt/usersofmentalhealthservices2004.cfm

Healthcare Commission 2005, *Survey of Users of Mental Health Services 2005*, Commission for Healthcare Audit and Inspection, London.

Healthcare Commission 2008a, *Survey of Users of Mental Health Services 2008*, Commission for Healthcare Audit and Inspection, London. Retrieved 11 September 2008 from http://www.healthcarecommission.org.uk/healthcareproviders/nationalfindings/surveys/healthcareproviders/surveysofpatients/mentalhealth.cfm

Healthcare Commission 2008b, *The pathway to recovery A review of NHS acute inpatient mental health services*, Commission for Healthcare Audit and Inspection, London. Retrieved 26 November 2008 from http://www.healthcarecommission.org.uk/publicationslibrary.cfm?fde_id=1197

Healthcare Commission 2008c, *Count me in 2008: Results of the 2008 national census of inpatients in mental health and learning disability services in England and Wales*, Commission for Healthcare Audit and Inspection, London. Retrieved 1 December 2008 from http://www.healthcarecommission.org.uk/_db/_documents/Count_me_in_census_2008_Results_of_the_national_census_of_inpatients_in_mental_health_and_learning_disability_services.pdf

Healy, D. 2005, *Psychiatric Drugs Explained*, 4th edn, Elsevier Churchill Livingstone, London.

Hill, A., Hardy, P. & Shepherd, G. 1996, *Perspectives on Manic Depression*, Sainsbury Centre for Mental Health, London.

Holmes, G. & Hudson M. 2006, *An evaluation of a Thinking about Medication Group*. Retrieved 23 December 2007 from http://www.shropsych.org/evaluationmeds.pdf

House of Commons Health Committee 2005, *The Influence of the Pharmaceutical Industry*, Stationery Office, Norwich.

Information Centre 2005, *Prescription Cost Analysis 2004*, Information Centre, Leeds. Retrieved 17 September 2008 from http://www.ic.nhs.uk/webfiles/publications/costanalysis05/PrescriptionCostAnalysis080405_PDF.pdf

Information Centre 2008, *Prescription Cost Analysis 2007*, Information Centre, Leeds. Retrieved on 17 July 2008 from http://www.ic.nhs.uk/statistics-and-data-collections/primary-care/prescriptions/prescription-cost-analysis-2007

Johnstone, L. 2000, *Users and Abusers of Psychiatry*, Routledge, London.

Jones, P. B., Barnes, T. R. E, Davies, L., Dunn, G., Lloyd, H., Hayhurst, K. P., Murray, R. M., Markwick, A. & Lewis, S. W. 2006, 'Randomized Controlled Trial of the Effect on Quality of Life of Second- vs First-Generation Antipsychotic Drugs in Schizophrenia', *Archives of General Psychiatry*, 63(10), pp. 1079–87. Retrieved 15 September 2008 from http://archpsyc.ama-assn.org/cgi/content/full/63/10/1079

Kimish, S. 2001, 'SMT...by a Recovering MD', in MHF, *Something Inside So Strong: Strategies for surviving mental distress*, Mental Health Foundation, London, pp. 97–8.

Kirsch, I., Deacon, B., Huedo-Medina, T., Scoboria, A., Moore, T. & Johnson, B. 2008, 'Initial Severity and Antidepressant Benefits: A Meta-Analysis of Data Submitted to the Food and Drug Administration', *PLoS Medicine*. Retrieved 19 May 2008 from http://medicine.plosjournals.org/perlserv/?request=getdocument&doi=10.1371%2Fjournal.pmed.0050045

Kramer, D. P. 1993, *Listening to Prozac: A psychiatrist explores antidepressant drugs and the remaking of self*, Viking Press, Northampton.

Kutchins, H. & Kirk, S. 1999, *Making Us Crazy: DSM – the psychiatric Bible and the creation of mental disorders*, Constable, London.

Lacey, R. & Woodward, S. 1985, *That's Life! Survey on tranquillisers*, BBC, London.

Lakhani, K. 2007, 'Special Report: Prescription Medicines', *Independent on Sunday*, 21 October. Retrieved 21 October 2007 from http://news.independent.co.uk/health/article3081840.ece

Law, J. 2006, *Big Pharma: How the world's biggest drug companies control illness*, Constable, London.

Layard, R. 2005, *Mental Health: Britain's biggest social problem?*, Centre for Economic Performance, London School of Economics, London. Retrieved 23 July 2007 from http://cep.lse.ac.uk/research/mentalhealth

Lester, H. & Glasby, J. 2006, *Mental Health Policy and Practice*, Palgrave Macmillan, Basingstoke.

Medawar, C. 1992, *Power and Dependence: Social audit on the safety of medicines*, Social Audit, London.

Medicines Guides. Retrieved 1 September 2008 from http://medguides. medicines.org.uk/document.aspx?name=Citalopram%20hydrochloride& preparation=1&use=Depression&section=sideEffects

MHAC 2005, *Count Me In: The National Mental Health and Ethnicity Census 2005 Service User Survey*, Mental Health Act Commission, Nottingham.

MHF 1997, *Knowing Our Own Minds*, Mental Health Foundation, London.

MHRA 2008, 'GSK investigation concludes', Medicines and Healthcare products Regulatory Agency, London, 2008. Retrieved 21 May 2008 from http://www. mhra.gov.uk/NewsCentre/Pressreleases/CON014152

Mind 2007, *Ecotherapy: The green agenda for mental health, Executive summary*, Mind, London. Retrieved 25 July 2007 from http://www.mind.org.uk/ mindweek/report

Moncrieff, J. 2006, 'Why is it so difficult to stop psychiatric drug treatment? It may be nothing to do with the original problem', *Medical Hypotheses*, 67(3), pp. 517–23.

Moncrieff, J. 2007, *The Myth of the Chemical Cure: A critique of psychiatric drug treatment*, Palgrave Macmillan, Basingstoke.

New Zealand Mental Health Commission 2001, *Recovery Competencies for New Zealand Mental Health Workers*, New Zealand Mental Health Commission, Wellington. Retrieved 18 August 2008 from http://www.mhc.govt.nz/publi-cations/documents/show/37–recovery-competencies-for-new-zealand-mental-health-workers

NICE 2002a, *Schizophrenia – atypical antipsychotics: Information for the public*, NICE, London.

NICE 2002b, *Treating and managing schizophrenia (core interventions). Understanding NICE guidance – information for people with schizophrenia, their advocates and carers, and the public*, NICE, London.

NICE 2003, *Schizophrenia: Full national clinical guideline on core interventions in primary and secondary care*, Gaskell and the British Psychological Society, London and Leicester, 2006. Retrieved 30 November 2007 from http://www. nice.org.uk/guidance/index.jsp?action=download&o=29033

NICE 2004a, *Zaleplon, zolpidem and zopiclone for insomnia. Information for people with insomnia, their families and carers, and the public*, NICE, London.

NICE 2004b, *Depression: Management of depression in primary and secondary care*, British Psychological Society and Gaskell, London and Leicester. Retrieved 24 December 2007 from http://www.nice.org.uk/guidance/index. jsp?action=download&o=29617

NICE 2005a, *A guide to NICE*, Retrieved 17 July 2007 from http://www.nice.org. uk/page.aspx?o=guidetonice

NICE 2005b, *Treating obsessive-compulsive disorder (OCD) and body dysmorphic disorder (BDD) in adults, children and young people. Understanding NICE guid-ance – information for people with OCD or BDD, their families and carers, and the public*, NICE, London.

NICE 2005c, *Post-traumatic stress disorder (PTSD): the treatment of PTSD in adults and children. Understanding NICE guidance – information for people with PTSD, their advocates and carers, and the public*, NICE, London.

NICE 2006a, *Bipolar disorder. Understanding NICE guidance- Information for people who use NHS services*, NICE, London.

NICE 2006b, Dementia: Understanding NICE guidance, NICE, London.

NICE 2007a, *Management of panic disorder and generalised anxiety disorder in adults. Understanding NICE guidance – information for people with panic disorder or generalised anxiety disorder, their families and carers, and the public*, NICE, London.

NICE 2007b, *The treatment of depression in adults. Understanding NICE guidance – information for people with depression, their advocates and carers, and the public*, NICE, London.

NICE 2009a, NICE, London. Retrieved 3 February 2009 from http://www.nice.org.uk/guidance/index.jsp?action=download&o=43042

NICE 2009b, *Medicines Adherence: Involving patients in decisions about prescribed medicines and supporting adherence: Full guidance*, National Collaborating Centre for Primary Care, and Royal College of General Practitioners, London. Retrieved 3 February 2009 from http://www.nice.org.uk/Guidance/CG76/Guidance/pdf/English

NICE n.d., *About clinical guidance*. Retrieved 5 September 2008 from http://www.nice.org.uk/aboutnice/whatwedo/aboutclinicalguidelines/about_clinical_guidelines.jsp

NIMHE 2003, *Inside Outside: Improving mental health services for black and minority ethnic communities in England*, National Institute for Mental Health in England, Leeds. Retrieved 3 September 2008 from www.chssc.salford.ac.uk/pdf/Insideoutside.pdf

NIMHE 2007, 'Huge funding boost to psychological therapy services'. Retrieved 2 November 2007 from http://www.mhchoice.csip.org.uk/

Norfolk, Suffolk and Cambridgeshire Strategic Health Authority 2003, *Independent Inquiry into the death of David Bennett*, Norfolk, Suffolk and Cambridgeshire Strategic Health Authority, Cambridge. Retrieved 3 August 2007 from http://www.blackmentalhealth.org.uk/main/index.php?option=com_content&task=blogcategory&id=23&Itemid=45

NSF n.d.(a), *A Question of Choice*, National Schizophrenia Fellowship, London.

NSF n.d.(b), *That's Just Typical*, National Schizophrenia Fellowship, London.

Panorama 2001, *The Tranquilliser Trap*, BBC, 13 May. Transcript retrieved 18 July 2007 from http://news.bbc.co.uk/hi/english/static/audio_video/programmes/panorama/transcripts/transcript_13_05_01.txt

Panorama 2003, *Seroxat: E-mails from the Edge*, BBC, 11 May. Transcript retrieved 3 July 2007 from http://news.bbc.co.uk/nol/shared/spl/hi/programmes/panorama/transcripts/emailsfromtheedge.txt

Paton, C., Barnes, T. R. E., Cavanagh, M.-R., Taylor, D. & Lelliott, P. 2008, 'High dose and combination antipsychotic prescribing in acute adult wards in the

UK: the challenges posed by p.r.n. prescribing', *British Journal of Psychiatry*, 192, pp. 435–9.

POMH UK 2008, Untitled. Retrieved 1 December 2008 from http://www.rcpsych.ac.uk/crtu/centreforqualityimprovement/prescribingobservatory.aspx

Postgraduate Medical Education and Training Board, *PMETB Briefing: The patients' role in healthcare: Challenges for the future*, 2008, London. Retrieved 12 August 2008 from http://www.pmetb.org.uk/fileadmin/user/Content_and_Outcomes/FD_briefings/Patients__Role_in_Healthcare_-_Summary_Sheet__Final.pdf

Quayle, F., Riding, S., Swift, N. & Savage, T. 2008, 'Audit of antidepressant prescribing in two practices in Shropshire County Primary Care Trust', unpublished.

Raleigh, V. S., Irons, R., Hawe, E., Scobie, S., Cook, A., Reeves, R., Petruckevitch, A. & Harrison, J. 2007, 'Ethnic variations in the experiences of mental health service users in England', *British Journal of Psychiatry*, 191, pp. 304–12.

Read, J. 2001, 'Involving to empower', *Mental Health Today*, December, Brighton.

Read, J. 2005, *Coping with Coming Off*, Mind, London.

Read, J. & Wallcraft, J. 1994, *Guidelines on advocacy for mental health workers*, Mind/Unison, London.

Redwood, H. 2001, 'Advertising Prescription Drugs Direct to Patients', *Health and Age*. Retrieved 17 September 2008 from http://www.healthandage.com/Home/gm=20!gid2=1633

Rethink 2006, *side effects*, London.

Rogers, A., Pilgrim, D. & Lacey, R. 1993, *Experiencing Psychiatry: Users' views of services*, Macmillan, Basingstoke.

Romme, M. & Escher, S. 1993, *Accepting Voices*, Mind, London.

Royal College of Psychiatrists 2008, *Fair Deal for Mental Health*, Royal College of Psychiatrists, London. Retrieved 18 August 2008 from http://www.rcpsych.ac.uk/campaigns/fairdeal.aspx

Russo, J. 2001, 'Reclaiming Madness', in MHF, *Something Inside so Strong: Strategies for surviving mental distress*, Mental Health Foundation, London, pp. 36–9.

SAMH 2004, *'All you need to know?'*, Scottish Association for Mental Health, Glasgow.

SCMH 2002, *Breaking the Circles of Fear*, Sainsbury Centre for Mental Health, London.

SCIE 2007, *A Common Purpose: Recovery in future mental health services*, Social Care Institute for Excellence, London.

Shapiro, K. & Shapiro, E. 1997, *The Powerful Placebo*, Johns Hopkins University Press, Baltimore.

Shaw, J., Hunt, S. M., Flynn, S., Meehan, J., Robinson, J., Bickley, H., Parsons, R., McCann, K., Burns, J., Amos, T., Kapur, N. & Appleby, L. 2006, 'Rates of mental disorder in people convicted of homicide', *British Journal of Psychiatry*, 188, pp. 143–7.

Slater, L. 2004, *Opening Skinner's Box: Great psychological experiments of the 20th century*, Bloomsbury, London.

Snowden, A. 2008, *Prescribing and Mental Health Nursing*, Quay Books, London.

Social Audit 2003, 'The Antidepressant Web'. Retrieved 27 October 2008 from http://www.socialaudit.org.uk/#The%20Antidepressant%20Web

Stagnitti, M. N. 2007, *Trends in the Use and Expenditures for the Therapeutic Class Prescribed Psychotherapeutic Agents and All Subclasses, 1997 and 2004: Statistical Brief No.163*, Agency for Healthcare Research and Quality, Rockville, Maryland. Retrieved 16 September 2008 from http://www.meps.ahrq.gov/mepsweb/data_stats/Pub_ProdResults_Details.jsp?pt=Statistical%20Brief&opt=2&id=803

Stagnitti, M. N. 2008, *Antidepressants Prescribed By Medical Doctors in Office Based and Outpatient Settings by Specialty for the U.S. Civilian Noninstitutionalized Population, 2002 and 2005: Statistical Brief No.206*, Agency for Healthcare Research and Quality, Rockville, Maryland. Retrieved 16 September 2008 from http://www.meps.ahrq.gov/mepsweb/data_files/publications/st206/stat206.pdf

Survivor/User History Group 2008, at http://studymore.org.uk/mpu.htm

Taylor, D., Paton, C. & Kerwin, R. 2007, *The Maudsley Prescribing Guidelines*, 9th edn, Informa Healthcare, London.

Taylor, P. J. & Gunn, J. 1999, 'Homicides by people with mental illness: Myth and reality', *British Journal of Psychiatry*, 174, pp. 9–14.

Thomas, A., Katsabouris, G. & Bouras, N. 1997, 'Staff perception on reduction of medication in patients with chronic schizophrenia', *Psychiatric Bulletin*, 21, pp. 692–4.

Thomas, P. & May, R. 2003, *Advice on Medication*, Hearing Voices Network, Manchester.

Tungaraza, T. & Poole, R. 2007, 'Influence of drug company authorship and sponsorship on drug trial outcomes', *British Journal of Psychiatry*, 191, pp. 82–3.

Turner, T. H. 2004, 'Long-term outcome of treating schizophrenia', *British Medical Journal*, 329, pp. 1058–9.

Vandenbroucke, J. P. 2004, 'Benefits and harms of drug treatments', *British Medical Journal*, 329, pp. 2–3.

Wallcraft, J., Read, J. & Sweeney, A. 2003, *On Our Own Terms*, Sainsbury Centre for Mental Health, London.

Watkins, J. 2006, *Healing Schizophrenia: Using medication wisely*, Michelle Anderson Publishing, Melbourne and London.

Whitaker, R. 2004, 'The case against antipsychotic drugs: A 50-year record of doing more harm than good', *Medical Hypotheses*, 62, pp. 5–13.

Index